PRIMAL
NEUROANTHROPOLOGY©
A Neuro-Sports Hypothesis

PRIMAL

NEUROANTHROPOLOGY©

A Neuro-Sports Hypothesis

Kenneth Bruce Van Gross, M.D.
Fusion Clinical Multimedia, Inc.

IPBOOKS.net
International Psychoanalytic Books

International Psychoanalytic Books (IPBooks)
New York • IPBooks.net

International Psychoanalytic Books (IPBooks)
Queens, New York
Online at: www.IPBooks.net

Cover design by Kathy Kovacic, Blackthorn Studio
Book design and back cover by Dan Williams

ISBN: 978-1-94-909339-1

Printed in the United States of America

Contents

Preface
2019: The Evolution of Neuroanthropology

Since the Primal Neuroanthropology of Sports hypothesis was born some twenty years ago, Neuroanthropology in general has evolved as a critical field in appreciating the human condition.

Noteworthy are recent papers by Bruner and Diederich who cite the neuroanthropological basis for Alzheimer's and Parkinson's disease (AD and PD) respectively.

Bruner makes the point that our overdeveloped parietal lobes became more susceptible to metabolic demands and thus are distinguished by their universally noted impairment in Alzheimer's disease.

Diederich suspects Parkinson's disease also is a consequence of human brain evolution. He cites the drag on the basal ganglia by a super developed human telencephalon (cerebral cortex) with the result being a higher likelihood for the basal ganglia degeneration noted in Parkinson's disease.

Inevitability of failure to our overly taxed cholinergic and dopaminergic systems also contributes to the AD and PD presentations. There may be more hypoxic sensitivity to cholinergic systems as a function of our vascular neuroanatomy and evolutionarily dictated under representation of substantia nigra based dopamine producing cells.

So the 2019 question of sports as a neuroanthropological entity has taken on new dimensions. In what way does it attest to our evolution in this highly complex world of games and sports? I would maintain we "hearken back" in some of the behaviors and automatic movements noted in sports. This indeed may have neuroanthropological signatures in our neuroanatomy, neurophysiology and neurochemistry. However, it has been our supremely developed cerebral cortices that constructed sports' forerunners and sports themselves with the implicit utilization of natural movements, postures, tendencies and habits.

At the same time, sports reflects neogenesis and neurodegeneration. It is the task of this volume to introduce some of that ideation which will hopefully allow for a great expansion of this athletic "field of dreams" we have integrated into human society as if it is air or sunlight.

Introductory Remarks and
"Facing" Some Emotional Issues

Classic views of tennis players winning big matches reveal multiple facets of our primal neurological nature. The player is often seen screaming, mouth wide open, eyes shut, head, neck and trunk extended, arms raised to the sky/heavens/outer universe/; he has let go of the tree branch as his hands are slightly flexed at the fingers while his racquet falls to his left and his arms slightly flexed left greater than right at the elbow.

The victorious player looks like he has landed. His knees are flexed as his quad muscles ripple and hip extensors contract while his toes hit the ground with his right sole not yet flush on the surface. This posture is exemplary of our Primal Neuroanthropology.

Hunting is essential to our primitive selves. The Kenyan tribesman hunts with the same kind of bow and arrow used by our ancestors thousands of years ago. He can be seen moving forward, shoulders square to his target, in the same way that a running back breaks into the line; his knees and trunk are slightly flexed as he prepares to shoot on the run at his moving prey; his tennis stance would be open and it is the equivalent of a forehand that he would indeed be preparing with the retraction of the arrow. We will attack these dynamics as this work unfolds; but first let us return to our primitive nature.

Vision is our most complex sense. In contrast to the rat and the cat, ape and man's visual superiority is based on the maintenance of binocular vision by the crossing of visual hemi-fields prior to processing in the visual cortex of the brain. Obviously, the hunter used such visual skills to aid him in his predatory missions.

In the hunting world, the eyes discover fearful situations. Monkeys photographed in Cayo Santiago, off the coast of Puerto Rico, exhibit our ancestral basis for facial behaviors made in response to fear- which includes freezing and teeth display.

Why are yawns "infectious" within groups of humans? A yawn is a display of a primitive greeting or acknowledgement, signified by the mandrill. The savanna baboon can show an exaggerated yawn in a weaponry display, flared nostrils and closure of the eyes. Why? Is sleep, with eye closure and yawning, linked primitively with displays of anger and fear which are often paired with screaming- and is that "infectious" yawn really a primitive interactive behavior either part of a more friendly greeting or less friendly agonist-antagonist covert and subconscious conversation characteristic of the yawn a human fetus will show on ultrasound? Is that our first ontogeny recapitulating phylogeny greeting?

There is progression in complexity of the facial muscles from rhesus monkey to orangutan to human. Our faces reveal our inner selves, our feelings conscious and unconscious and facial expressions form a channel of communication between parent and child with smiling and other facial expressions reinforcing the bond between parent and baby- the key to displays of anger and ecstasy. A social smile, appearing at 3-4 months, has ties to ""snarl mimicry " noted between mother and child apes and a fixed or painted smile in humans is actually a sign of an adversarial agenda so snarling and smiling can be emotionally linked. The left side of the face would appear to be more expressive for certain emotions than the right.

Head weaving in the cercopithecus cephus monkey is also called flagging- momentary yet repeated monitoring of the object of display. Smooth pursuits may well have their primitive tie to these movements; isn't this kind of tracking so critical in, for example, the playing of center field?

Prefrontal cortex, hypothalamus, hippocampus and amygdala are all key regions in our brains and in those of our primate ancestors engaged in predatory activities in the wild. As danger is processed cortically and ultimately analyzed by the prefrontal cortex, a neuroendocrine response is generated in the hypothalamus. A learned behavior component is drawn upon from the hippocampus and the danger/rage center (amygdala) is activated. The teeth display is in response to danger; the unleashing of the primitive two handed open stanced backhand is perhaps as instinctive a stroke in our repertoire. The amygdala is our competition trigger on the tennis court and on other athletic fields.

Other components of the limbic system from which the prefrontal cortex, hypothalamus, hippocampus and amygdala are parts are also important in generating the behaviors just outlined include the thalamus, a sensory relay station and pituitary, the neuroendocrine reservoir. The hippocampus is part of the temporal lobe which is our primary memory bank. The prefrontal and frontal lobe regions are our signature primitive human brain components for they were what directed us to "let go of the branch" and assume a bipedal posture alluded to earlier. The frontal lobes are our executors; they provided us with anxiety about hanging on to that branch indefinitely and motivate us to let go and achieve that bipedalism. Frontal lobotomy patients become apathetic which provides another way to understand how the frontal lobes cognitively drive us.

Locomotion and Primitive
Lip/Tongue Movements

Our ancestors swung from branches via five main types of primate locomotion; vertical clinging and leaping, arboreal quadrupedalism, terrestrial quadrupedalism, brachiation and bipedalism. We are the only primate that moves bipedally and erect. But we are also capable of reaching into our primitive past to assume these other postures. In fact, athletically, as will be noted, we often can adopt these other postures to our advantage and in effect assert our evolutionary heritage. Interestingly, recent research suggests some of our monkey ancestors walked semi-erect from the branches from which they were swinging.

The following are some theoretical underpinnings for bipedal locomotion: carrying, weapon and tool use, travelling, bush and tree reaching for food and family provisioning. Sports analogies are quite apparent. Simultaneously with carrying and transferring with the hands was the walking/running motion with feet; thus, the primal neuroanthropological basis for dribbling a soccer ball can be conceptualized. Recently, a Turkish clan was discovered by Tan to possess what may be a reverse evolution gene. The family walked on all fours! Our hunt driven ancestors undoubtedly slithered through the forest on their bellies.

Bipedal walking and running are energetically efficient ways for a large primate such as the human to travel long distances easily and perform bursts of short distance activity such as hunting. Soccer in fact is characterized by a long relatively slow trot that tests endurance interspersed with these bursts of goal directed attacks where speed is critical.

It is instructive to note that a bipedal posture with truncal and knee flexion is the posture of the chimpanzee. This would also be our post- tree descent posture. When one considers the sports injuries to the back and knee that relate to hyperextension and evolutionary and mechanically sports ideal flexed postures, we must wonder whether a fully erect posture is in fact our natural destiny. Look at the elderly stooped forward to their natural advantage as posterior compromise of the spinal canal by osteophytes sets in promoting forward flexion. Our bony decline leads us to the return to fetal flexion. And yet there is a center of mass issue that would incline us to perform certain sports in more fully erect postures- running track or basketball sprinting are examples.

However, as far as energy for walking and running, many other animals exceed our economy. Apparently, we are not on this earth simply to exhibit efficient locomotion.

Postures are one clue to our primate heritage and the

way we degenerate. Lip movements are another. Again, ontogeny also recapitulates phylogeny. Additionally, degeneration recapitulates ontogeny and phylogeny.

There is a pathological reflex noted in the demented elderly called the suck reflex. Aging in fact recapitulates ontogeny as this reflex recalls the rooting of the infant on the mother's breast. Now prior to our dementing (which also often includes regressive reflexes like grasping and nasal flaring, we recapitulate this act with movements like lip smacking when we anticipate some good food or biting when we get aroused during sex or boxing matches and of course the most pervasive recapitulation- smoking- where the handling of the cigarette, cigar or pipe followed by lip stimulation, sucking and inhaling is legendary.) Of interest is the fact that the moving of the smoked object away from the face and the backhanded match lighting simulates the movements of the tennis backhand- indeed our most primitive stroke. The smelling and tasting of the smoke is another primitive issue that I believe is tied to our primitive appreciation of fire and the strong motivational and memory characteristics of the smell/taste cortex.

Cooing can be seen in the monkeys described earlier in Puerto Rico which are frozen in fear. The lip position for cooing is also simulated by the kissing or sucking lip movements. Many believe cooing is a way to allay fear by hearkening back to breast sucking. Darwin believed smiling was the equivalent of the cooing antagonistic muscles of the face- the post-suck satisfying facial muscle action (smiling and sucking controlled by Cranial Nerve 7) interestingly we can smile while   losing the ability to volitionally create a smile, suggesting the "emotional brain" supersedes to some degree voluntary muscle control. There is also "pathological laughter" and "pathological crying" which are neurological syndromes where involuntary emotional responses dominate.

Why do we happen to have words such as "cool" to equate with a sought after behavior or "cuckoo"- to describe a kind of blissful insanity?- the whip-poor-will sings out- woo-woo..woo; again our simulation is with pursed/cooing approximated lips. Interestingly, the song of this bird is the background for the Rolling Stones' primitive "Ode to the Devil".

Tongue extension is noted during predatory responses in non-human primates. It is also a characteristic human trait in the course of intense concentration- perhaps related to the development of language which is in fact the extrusion of thoughts through a rich variation of sounds. Likewise, tongue extrusion is often part of human athletic movement expression. Of course, both the tongue and speech/language

4

centers have extensive representation within the lobes of the brain.

We subconsciously use the term "tongue-tied" to connect our unique tongue movements and vocal utterances with our humanness.

Lip smacking according to Montagu is the only sound that a mother baboon makes while grooming her infant- it seems to serve to reduce tension and promote tranquility in social interactions. Lip smacking is another commonly seen "regressive reflex" in the dementing elderly or in those with certain basal ganglia degenerations.

Cerebellum and
the Vestibular System

Originally felt to be exclusively a regulator of speed, intensity and direction of movement, the cerebellum is now appreciated as uniquely developed in humans, particularly in the key dentate nucleus. The cerebellum would appear to have an essential role in coordinating physical cues through which nonverbal communication occurs. The ability then to "read" an opponent on the tennis court in addition to the executing of a perfectly hit overhead are both in part cerebellar activities.

Our large cerebral cortex, which houses reasoning, abstract thought, memory and language, is audacious. Our fine dexterity is unique in the animal kingdom and relates to "touch" which for example is associated with the ability to hit a good drop shot in tennis. But imagine the Homo sapien in a quintessential human movement position- featuring the toe pointing and relatively erect posture but also exhibiting what I would call primordial reaching with the right arm in extension as if simulating reaching for the fruit on the tree or the follow through after the release of the arrow from the bow.

There are rich connections to the brain stem and the vestibular nerves via the cerebellum. All of this allows us to maintain balance regardless of our evolutionary state or activity. In addition there are balance links to eye movement coordination and gaze stability while we search for touchdown pass receivers or birds to shoot down.

Vertigo- the sensation of spinning motion can be induced by games of sliding, swinging, twirling and jumping. Tumbling is clearly in the mix as well as a vertigo inducer. Nowadays, we can point to gymnastics, childhood swings, the merry-go-round and outdoor sports such as skiing and mountain climbing, but in fact to any sport for that matter. Wasn't it the intensely emotive sportscaster Marv Albert who always described the movements of Earl Monroe, the great basketball player, as "spinning, spinning, spinning...."?

Callois states that we have a fundamental tendency to feel the body's stability and equilibrium momentarily destroyed to escape the tyranny of perception and to overcome awareness.

Centrifugal and other balance disrupting movements allow us to attain an altered state, and as we all know, that state also often is part of a sense of giddiness or fun.

But how conscious are we for this giddiness tendency? Every mother knows intuitively that in order to put her baby to sleep she has to rock it thereby repeating the primordial dance of the fetus swaying in the womb. Rhythm and whirling take each of us back to reminiscences of nirvanic equanimity. Then as the baby ages, self-rocking is initiated. Among orthodox Jews and Arabs, body-rocking often accompanies prayer, grief and study. Amongst the mentally troubled, rocking is again self initiated, as is rocking and head banging in children with the sleep syndrome- Jacatio Capitus. It is comforting and likely is the basis for dances like the waltz, the Limbo Rock, the Twist and perhaps underlies the entire rock and roll genre.

Dr. Joseph Solomon has observed that patients taken from their rooms in hospital for transfer to another town by train, though they had earlier needed to be restrained in straitjackets and muffs, become very quiet and calm as soon as the train was in motion. Solomon reasons that this vestibular (balance center) stimulation has the effect of re- integrating a feeling of non-abandonment that infantile rocking offered by the mother was able to accomplish.

And yet rocking has some physiological benefits in its own right as noted by Montagu: It increases cardiac output and is helpful to the circulation; it promotes respiration and decreases lung congestion and stimulates muscle tone and gastrointestinal motility.

A thesis advanced here is that not only is balance altering motion (B.A.M.) a tendency that relates to the invention of fun games and allows us to hearken back to cradling, it is a drive the way sucking, feeding and sleeping are drives. After all- the mother rocking her baby is rocking herself!!!

Our drive to drive? Was it Pontiac that carried the slogan- "builds driving excitement"? Is that what our parents built within us when we were created? Do we have intrinsic evolutionary excitement potential related to our leap from trees in a way that constantly motivates us to seek simulated leaps or rushes of movement? And now can we better explain the paintings of tumblers on the cave wall in Tanzania or a falling hunter located on a cave painting in France?

The vestibular system has rich connections in the brain. There are strong links to the sleep center in the brain stem, particularly its critical site of REM or rapid eye movement sleep. Eye movement sleep- eye movement desensitization reprocessing has become a lynchpin for a new kind of psychotherapy highlighted by the induction of eye movements which seem to help purge traumatic thoughts from the patient's mind. Indeed, according to one theory, the function of dreams, noted predominantly in REM sleep, is to induce the same purging. Intriguingly, all muscle tone is lost during REM except that related to rapid horizontal eye movements and to erections. Given what Freud has taught us about sex and dreams, that neurophysiological aspect makes sense- likewise, darting vestibular system linked eye movements would also have that dream primality link. And the pervasive "falling dream": A fusion of sexual and vestibular issues? In fact the vestibular center is tied to a variety of eye movements some called saccadic or rapid focusing inducing movements, others called smooth pursuits which allows for monitoring and the third so called vestibular- ocular reflexes which allow for the maintenance of appropriate head and neck positions in the course of fixating on targets.

The vestibular center located in the brain stem, our most critically important brain center, located deep in the brain, which maintains respiration and impacts significantly on heart rate and blood pressure, also has ties to the cerebellar eye, hand, foot, body coordination center. In addition, there are key vestibular links to the basal ganglia, a deep brain center that refines movement speed, initiation and tone regulation. In addition, there are vestibular links to the cerebral cortex or thinking brain and to the spinal cord or railroad track for sensation and movement for the arms, legs and trunk.

So, we have established the fundamental role for a variety of gross primitive movements as they relate to sports particularly tennis and we have established the primal nature of B.A.M. and can understand how B.A.M. as a drive underlies much of sports such as tennis.

The Human Hand and Its Origins

However, we cannot neglect fine manipulative skills in the generation of the neuroanthropological basis for sports. Fine manipulative skills are hallmarks of the human species. Certainly one can appreciate these human hand grips in tool usage, but look how critical they are in the gripping of a baseball or a golf club or of course a tennis racquet? Finger flexion and finger rotation are keys to gripping and fine maneuvering of these finger movements allows for "touch" in sports like tennis or golf. Thumb rotation particularly distinguishes our human gripping ability from that of apes. In fact, if you note the ape holding on to the branch, he isn't even using his thumb at all. In addition, the cerebral cortex representation of the hand is heavily represented in primates, more than in any other species and particularly in man, where the thumb has the most representation compared to any other species.

The saddle joint in the chimp interlocks more, which restricts movement compared to that noted in man. However, we must think inferentially because fossil remains are largely bones, rarely peripheral nerves and never central nervous system remains.

What is the primitive basis for golf? Research suggests that thousands of years ago, upper Paleolithic toolmakers created a blade tool by standing over it holding a rod-like tool making device, right hand over left, with the rock being carved at the kind of level where the ball on a tee might be.

Wolfe has shown a near stationary proximal carpal row of wrist bones during the dart tosser's motion, which is believed to provide a stable platform for the generation of force and accuracy during certain power and precision grip activities. This formation may represent a divergence from apes, in synchrony with adaptation in the human hand to the manipulation of tools and central to the development of the human's unique ability to aim and accelerate tools and weapons.

Young has also noted that ape like curved fingers in primates were transformed into their current form featuring a large muscular opposable thumb and shorter straight fingers. Out of this came two new grips important in throwing and striking- a fingertip-pad throwing grip for hurling spheroidal missiles and a firm buttressed striking grip for grasping cylindrical club handles.

Thus, the hand is of great importance in the evolution of spear hunting and throwing.

Big Game Hunting, Playing and Throwing

Why is "big game hunting" called "game" hunting anyway? Hunting= game seeking; game = play so game seeking=play seeking; play= the B.A.M. drive so hunting is in effect a primitive drive as well. When the hyperflexed posture of the hunter is recalled, it is easy to conjure up the crouching at the net to hit a volley.

When the hunter threw his spear, one can imagine the origin of the serve.

Remove the spear and one still connects to throwing. What is also interesting is the use of a denticulate or a stone tool with a notched serrated edged, good to kill and maim animals. The denticulate connection also has links to dentition and the primal act of biting and fascinatingly, the distinguishing nucleus in the human cerebellum in the shape of a tooth- the dentate nucleus.

Let us delve deeper into throwing: According to Calvin, the hominid discovery of the ability to throw overhand 50,000 years ago coincided with the development of language because the complex movement of throwing for distance with accuracy and speed requires the recruitment of many thousands of neurons and with doubling and tripling of distances, the number of neurons required is multiplied exponentially. For example, hitting a rabbit with a rock thrown from one car length away requires several thousand neurons working in synch. If you go to 2 and then 3 car lengths away, you require 64 and then 729 times as many neurons respectively. According to Calvin, just as the complexities of language required us to have a larger brain, so too did the complexities of specialized throwing require us to have larger brains.

According to Calvin, the planning of ballistic movements, that is extremely rapid actions of the limbs that once initiated cannot be modified, may have led to a quantum leap in the size of the human brain. Only chimpanzees can simulate human throwing (though only underhanded); they also have an idea about throwing as a threat. Gorillas and monkeys don't throw; shoulder structure also limits them.

Calvin also recognizes hitting a baseball as a ballistic movement which the brain must plan before commencing the action. By extension, one would include the tennis groundstrokes, particularly two handed strokes into this model. Obviously, clubbing for food or defeating one's enemy is the primitive human neuroanthropological movement that predates ball striking.

What is also interesting is that the term throwing constantly has primal connotations such as "throwing up" (vomiting), "throwing in the towel" (surrendering), "throwing big" (whimsical decision making) "throw in this or that item" (randomly assigning or doing something semi-purposively, kind of destiny driven behavior), "caste lots" (again throwing tied to a result out of our control) "throw this idea out to you" (an implied chance-tied toss of fate). The concept that throwing is an instinct is very provocative in these idioms, which reflect an unconscious acknowledgement of our evolution.

Reaching prior to a ballistic arm movement characterizes not only the overhand throw seen in the baseball pitch but the serving motion in tennis. The rock fling, the spear toss and the arrow sling all serve as the basis for these actions.

Neuroanatomically, the Subthalamic Nucleus of Luys is key to all of our hemiballistic movements, as a lesion of this nucleus (which is paired deep in the brain on either side of the midline and as the name implies is below the thalamus) will induce a flailing purposeless involuntary throwing motion usually of the arm opposite to the side of the lesion. It would be of great interest to measure the relative sizes of the Subthalamic Nucleus of Luys in other primates and to determine if in fact anything comparable exists throughout the animal kingdom.

To be clear about dates, whereas proto-language and non-overhead throwing may have begun more than a million years ago, spear throwing probably began about 50,000 years ago, bow and arrow use about 12,000 years ago and slings about 5000 years ago when David slew Goliath. Parenthetically, it is also noteworthy that the Talmud goes into major detail about no throwing laws on the Sabbath, connecting throwing with the prohibition against transferring anything on the Sabbath and elevating throwing to a major Sabbath taboo in line with this concept that throwing is in part a type of critical if not sentinel evolutionary behavior.

Young has studied the ontogeny of throwing and striking and reports that throwing and striking are predominantly the result of an inherited motor program, not improved upon by instruction and carry a prominent gender difference, with boys superior to girls in speed and power of throwing and striking.

Weapons and Strokes

An 8,000-year-old painting from Turkey depicts a running hunter. The picture evokes the pulling back of the tennis racket to serve or strike a forehand.

Bushmen still hunt with bow and arrows. Their crouches suggest the position assumed at the net to strike a volley.

So there are several images that expand the links from hunting to sports. Here we note the evolution of improved gaming equipment. Cord linked spears enhanced ballistic power of Cro-Magnon man. The cord attached to the spear allowed him to throw spears from 70 to 150 yards. Compare the power of the old wooden racquets with the new graphite models- modern day equivalents to spear thrower attachments.

With the advent of advanced weaponry and costumes, the hunt evolved to spectacle, whether it became the tournament hype of a grand slam tennis event or a Mochica hunter of the classic period of Peruvian prehistory (0-500 AD). According to illustrations from that period, hunters wore elaborate garb (uniforms) and the painted face. (today's shoe polish below the eyes?). The high arching forehand back swing or overhand serve arm cocking was inferred in the Peruvian warrior's posturing as was the primal toe/heel combination involving the right and left feet. Hunting and war art depicted the protagonist with the weapon in his right hand- apparently the "achievement or goal directed side".

In drawings from the 1700's, the right hand is shown as the holder of the kill weapon in Hawaiian battle scenes from that era. The spear carriers are shown holding their weapons in the traditional right- handed style of right hand on top. The crouched posture of the foreground killer is noted in the depiction, with the arm raised as if in the middle of an overhead smash.

Clubbing was shown in the same illustration as a right-handed action, a kind of two handed right sided serving motion.

In primitive plowing scenes from present day Kenya, the origins of golf and hockey are suggested. Certainly, handedness with the plow would be carried over to handedness with weapons of destruction, as motor strength would need to be optimized in both clubbing to kill and digging as deeply as possible into the ground.

Right-handed warriors either throw their spears or wield them like clubs. African hunters, hovering over their wildlife kill, are reminiscent of the "sack dance" of New York Jet defensive end Mark Gastineau after he had thrown the quarterback to the ground.

A New Guinea Gimi in "warrior uniform" crouches over his "prey" holding his weapon in his right hand. The warrior will play act the hunt, using a right handed bow and arrow posture and a ""strut"" which evokes immodesty about warrior status and the posturing of a Dion Sanders after scoring a touchdown.

Masai warriors burst into a running dance celebrating their unity as fighters. Again there is right-handed domination of spear and flag carrying.

The Tanganyikan hunter helps support the thesis that the open forehand, particularly the running open forehand is the shot of choice in tennis; forward motion while spear throwing is best accomplished when the hunter is square to his target.

And yet the open stance forehand can hardly be called the only "instinctive" stance, implicated by recognizing the large number of outstanding closed stance tennis pros (Stan Smith, a top U.S. pro in the 70's comes to mind as a leading closed stance player). The other key point is that given the luxury of planting oneself, many people will maximize their power potential by adopting a closed stance. These are people for whom a classic technique of weight shifting to the back right foot followed by a shift to the left foot that peaks at ball impact is ideal. The tennis serve works well with a closed stance as does the golf shot, the baseball swing or the quarterback fling. All of these activities involve adopting a stationary starting position.

The sub-Saharan hunter takes his looping forehand lion catching spear "cross court or in position to hit a line drive down the left field line". The angle he decides to position himself at to spear his prey is quite similar to what would be the angle that can be drawn from home plate to the "pull field" (left) of a Close stance right sided power hitter.

A young student on a tribal African hunting expedition with his father watches in the primal neuroanthropological "information processing" stance of trunk and knee flexion with hands placed on thighs. Recall the outfielder assuming this stance while he processes the visual information conveyed by the pitcher-batter scene in front of him or the football team huddled in this stance while processing the verbal information given them by the quarterback.

The Left-Right Story

The Kenyan hunter, who might shoot his arrow left handed, is at the same time adopting a right handed backhand position. In fact, as is often instructed, the backhand is really the simpler stroke; the right arm in this case is, without much fanfare, poised for the initiation of the back swing. There is a strong subgroup of good right handed backhanders who can hit a "natural" left handed forehand (as dictated by a left handed bow and arrow user). Ivan Lendl comes to mind as a great backhander who "naturally" plays golf left-handed, which meanshis key lead arm is the right in "back hand" position.

Parenthetically, one of the reasons for golf problems in many is the fact that although the right-handed golf club held as a bat is a power tool with the right hand on top, it is less of a right-handed power and accuracy weapon when used as a golf club where the "lead" role of the left arm is so important in swing dynamics and shot placement. In fact, many of these golf "right-handers" need to be more "left-handed" to succeed in golf where coordination related accuracy is so much more important than it is in baseball. The explanation for the backhand, forehand and serve that is even more primordial than the throwing of spears or the use of bows and arrows may be as follows: Early man was faced with moving through shrub and branch obstructing jungle forests, irrespective of his animal hunting needs at the time. He needed to be an open stanced forehander, backhander and overhead motioned slasher as he moved these obstructions out of the way while he created pathways in front of him.

In his analysis of neuro-evolution, Calvin visualizes a right handed woman hunter carrying her infant in her left hand, near her comforting and beating heart. (Left-handed infant carrying is noted throughout the primate and monkey worlds). The left brain has of course the special facility for organizing the sequences of fine movement required for speech and skilled right hand control. The right brain is more spatially oriented and probably leads in postural and visual recognition control. How else can we fully explain the hemi-spatial difficulties so prominent only when the right brain is damaged?

Most of mankind is not fully left or right-handed but as we emerge from infancy, a preference for left or right is highly characteristic of humans. This will relate to certain pathological issues to be discussed below.

The term left or right side dominant is preferred for any given activity and need not be limited to the hands. The sidedness issue is critical to analyze in any given athlete as different athletic skills may be favored by different sides in the same person. There is also the issue of dorsal vs. volar preference, represented by varying abilities with backhand vs. forehand for a given arm, leg or hemi-trunk. (Long tract distribution, which is cortical representation of muscles based on their power, is an important co-consideration in defining a player's strengths.) It turns out that the branch holding to ground landing sequence of muscle usage indicates that the most critical muscles used in the sequence are given more cortical representation than their antagonistic adjacent muscle. In observing stroke victims, a stereotypical pattern of weakness is the rule for this reason.

The right hemisphere is the better expresser of emotion, particularly anger with snarling observed mostly with the left face.

But also of note is the fact that the right hemisphere appears to be a seat of self-awareness as damage to it not only can cause weakness or loss of vision in the opposite side, but loss of awareness that something is wrong with the opposite side. This phenomenon is not present when the left hemisphere is comparably damaged implying a pre-eminent role for self-awareness in the right hemisphere.

The left and right brain maintain crossed visual pathways, allowing us to maintain at least a portion of left or right sided vision despite injury to a single hemisphere. Hearing and smell to a lesser extent is preserved bilaterally even if one cortex is damaged. In the majority of humans, language is housed in the left hemisphere (including the basal ganglionic subcortex) whereas more spatial activities are localized in the right brain.

But this mute right brain has more intriguing proclivities. We have a tendency to place emotion-laden experience, particularly evil, mystical or taboo experience on our left side. This is noted in ancient Chinese paintings from the 4th century.

At the same time, the cold calculated goal directed throw is much more often a right-handed motion (Calvin of course ties it to coexisting development of language- also left brain or right handed). Left- handed throwers are often labeled tricky or inscrutable. Some possess a screwball, for some reason, rarely in the repertoire of a right hander. A screwball is of course also another name for a weirdo (in line with those "wacky" lefties).

Thus, sports, evolution and our brains are loaded with issues relating to left and right sidedness. Two salient points should be highlighted:

1. Dominance for one side for any individual (and for the species as a whole) or the other relates to the localization of certain functions that became highly developed in humans such as language and throwing.

2. Ambidexterity is not the rule for humans for motor skills that become increasingly refined. However, clear advantages exist in sport and in certain other activities such as hunting where the ability to "go both ways" can raise the level of ability to a still higher plane.

Basketball and Other Evolutionary Callings

Primal dunks suggest the leap to obtain hanging fruits on the vine followed by the facial expression of thrill upon accomplishing it. In equally primal fashion, the post-dunk basket rim hang takes us back to those first grasps of the branch prior to our bipedal landing while the exhibition of snarling and teeth displays are expressed.

Basketball can be viewed anthropologically as some kind of re- enactment involving the acquisition of food off trees and then passing the goods to others in the tribe.

One would imagine there was a great tendency to keep score of how many any one individual could garner. Perhaps there was a kind of March Madness tournament as spring sprang out there in Africa, during which competitors lined up in pairs to battle over fruit on a given tree. Losers might be sacrificed if not eaten by the victorious participants as the tourney progressed to a Final Not on all Fours Finale.

Expressions on the basketball court are legendary and often conjure up the snarling, grimacing, teeth displays and cooing noted above in our ancestors.

No one instructs lions, monkeys and other species to "exhibit a facial expression by opening your mouth and flaring your nostrils". The other aspect with this display is that it is perceived as hostile. Why is the animal kingdom programmed to perceive that facial pattern as hostile anyway? It may again return us to the frustrated open-mouthed newborn unable to find the primordial nipple on which to suck.

Mouth closure, if not lip pursing during hyper-attention is noted in primates and in sports playing humans such as NBA players. Why? It may relate to the "freezing" posture during threatening situations when angry displays of teeth are less important than determined concentration.

The pursed lips of golfer Tiger Woods is famous. The concentrating infant on the maternal breast would also utilize this pursing.

Teeth grinding is tied to hostility on the battlefield and in sports. Bracha has argued that during the early Paleolithic environment of evolutionary adaptedness, jaw clenching was an adaptive trait because it rapidly strengthened the masseter and temporalis muscles, enabling a stronger, deeper and therefore more lethal bite in expectation of conflict (warfare). Similarly, sharper incisors produced by teeth grinding may have served as weaponry during early human combat. We can posit that alleles predisposing to fear-induced clenching-grinding were evolutionarily conserved in the human clad (lineage) since they remained adaptive for anatomically and mitochondrially modern humans (Homo sapiens) well into the mid-Paleolithic period.

Teeth displays, as noted earlier can be part of smiling which of course need not always connote a friendly facial movement- this kind of mocking facial expression of smiling without being happy is seen in basketball, golf and many other sports where a player is in some way upset at his own performance, that of others, or punished for an illegal action. Where are referees in the jungle however? Perhaps since they weren't there, we had to invent them. They came to be known as gods or a god- purveyors of correct behavior

Facial behaviors of medal winners of the judo competition at the 2004 Athens Olympic Games were coded with P. Ekman and W. V. Friesen's Facial Affect Coding System (FACS) and interpreted using their Emotion FACS dictionary. Winners' spontaneous expressions were captured immediately when they completed medal matches, when they received their medal from a dignitary, and when they posed on the podium. The 84 athletes who contributed expressions came from 35 countries. The findings strongly supported the notion that expressions occur in relation to emotionally evocative contexts in people of all cultures, that these expressions correspond to the facial expressions of emotion considered to be universal, that expressions provide information that can reliably differentiate the antecedent situations that produced them, and that expressions that occur without inhibition are different than those that occur in social and interactive settings.

Nowadays, it is quite common to see players, upon hitting a home run or scoring a touchdown, to supplement facial expressions with looks and points to the heavens. Are they thanking the ultimate referee? (Note they will also at times look to the skies in petition after doing something wrong). Upgaze in Neurology is linked to Nirvana via a relation to falling off to sleep with our eyes rolling up.

Many athletes utter power grunts and groans. Monica Seles comes to mind. Of course, primal scream therapy, developed by Eric Fromm, is a therapy designed to unfetter the patient from the shackles of his conscious mind.

The fist pump is primal. Who is telling people who succeed in sports to use this gesture? I see it as our primal link to that penultimate tree branch grasp before we landed on our feet.

It would be unfair to label a gesture laden player like Jimmy Connors or others as "primitive", but in introducing sports movements as something more than "just being an animal", it would be fair to acknowledge that these players derive success from the unleashing of so called primitive movements. No one ever instructed Kevin Garnett or Dirk Nowitzki to snarl and show their teeth in "hostile display", but in the course of descending (off the tree branch?) with a rebound, this facial pattern is utilized, it would seem to energize the star player and to antagonize their opponents although the choice to utilize the facial musculature in this way is out of a player's consciousness. Here then is the sports link to our primal neuroanthropological roots.

Illustrations

Tumbling, diving, stroking and racing. The vast array of sports positions, motions and maneuvers.

Branch hanging begot landing bipedally.

Our biceps muscles for same hold are stronger and more represented in the brain than their antagonist extensors, the triceps.

The "primal scream" is apparent upon standing upright relying on the stronger quadriceps vs. their antagonists the hamstrings.

The phylogenic transmission of primal postures to athletes in the world of sports.

Hunting involved a fearlessness evident in the teeth display and grimace.

In addition, the weaponry is grasped while the costume of the hunt or of war is painted on the skin.

Weaponry developed as per this cave painting of old.

The bow and its arrow draw parallels the drawn back tennis racquet poised to swing forward to propel the ball-weapon that once was the arrow.

Target: the other side of the net, the opponent himself or the deer in ancient times.

Whether using the right hand, the left hand or both, the grasp became refined to handle weaponry as such tools became more sophisticated and able to be flung to prey yards away. For men, stabbing was and is characteristically overhand. For women, it has been usually performed underhanded. This is useful in forensic analysis even today.

Here is a woman hunter perhaps assigned to club a large mammal. The bat is still a powerful tool in softball and the force generated can slay the ball as it may have cracked the skull of what was to be lunch.

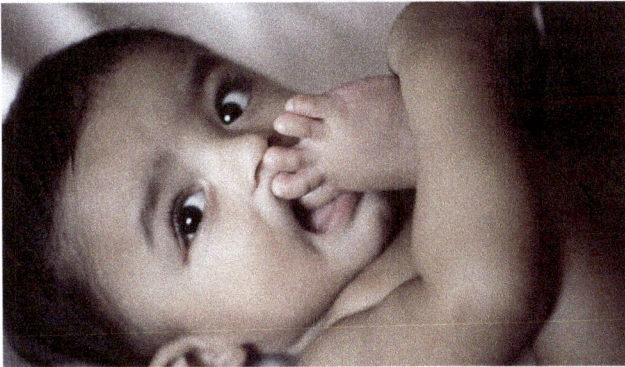

Fisting or foot sucking satisfies some oral needs and in turn is reflexive; the primitive suck reflex can be seen in lip pursing on the playing field, through tobacco chewing or the modern day habit of dangling a tooth retainer from the mouth in basketball.

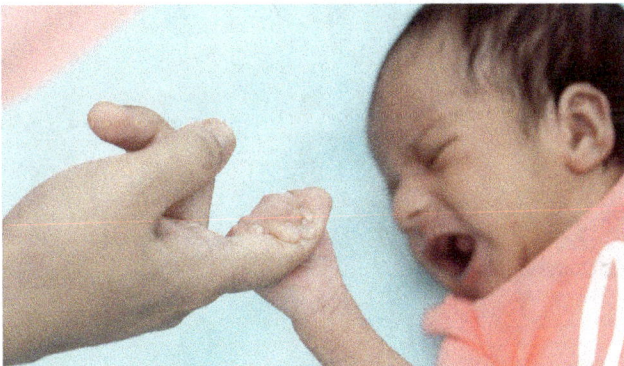

Resurfacing in man as we dement in late life, the grasp reflex is noted in this newborn. It reflects attachment to "tools of the trade" from a squash racquet handle to a curling broom for that Olympic sport.

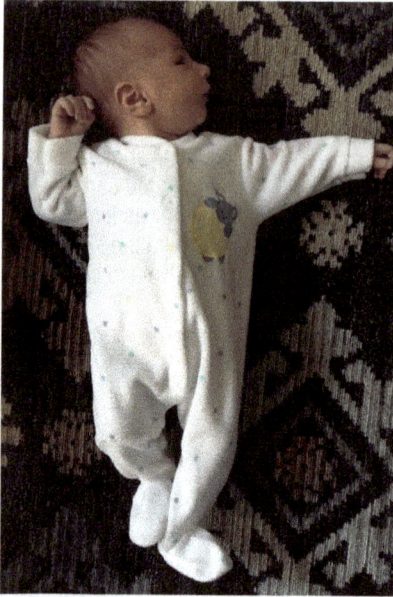

This is the "fencing posture" noted in the primitive reflex called the asymmetrical tonic neck reflex.

Here is its manifestation in the sport of fencing- one arm raised in flexion, the other arm held in extension.

Huddling fosters togetherness and teamwork whether in a monkey troop…

…Or within a soccer squad.

Ball in mouth probably began with mouth open in play excitement; the ball is a perfect fit.

Ball on ground and tongue out may be signifying satisfaction (as per Michael Jordan around the hoop).

Ontological evidence as the protruded tongue links to the concentration in this dribbling.

The tongue protrusion can also signify defiance or fear whether on the ball field or in the wild.

Modern day weapon of sports- the critical ground stroke called the forehand.

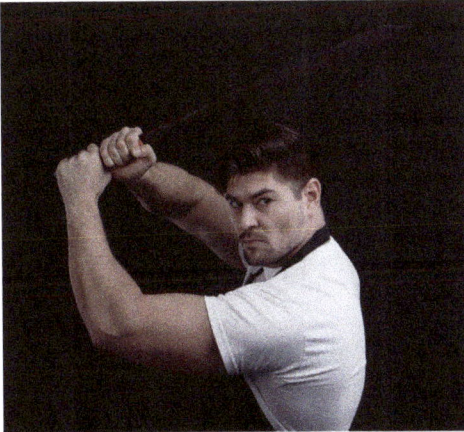

Machetes were used as the ground stroke forerunner; lashing and slashing in the jungle or in this mano a mano battle to the death.

Tahitian dance has some lashing with the hands along with, in some cases, shivering type movements with the fingers, fluid hand movements, hula type hip and feet movements and facial grimacing. The dance-sport connection is profound.

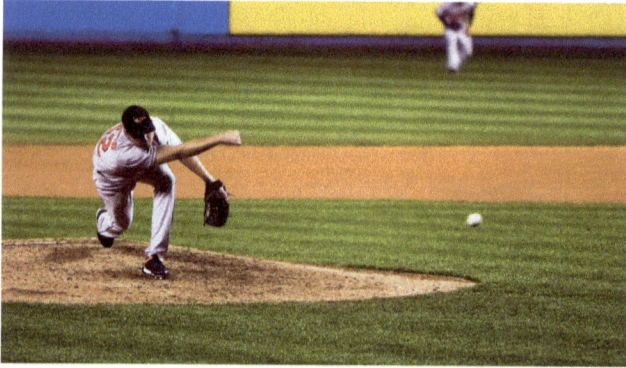

This pitch has corollary with the whip of the domesticated bull or cow in the field. It is not only seen (rarely) in professional baseball but a motion like it characterizes the swing in field hockey, ice hockey or softball pitching.

The overhand throw correlated with the development of human language. Long distance killing by way of rock or spear throwing overhand was noted about 50,000 years ago as more complex language began. It would seem that awareness of the ability to kill at a distance paralleled the realization that a few choice words could launch a battle or shut down an argument. On one hand, it became understood that targeted hunting and warring at a distance could be far more efficient than engaging in scuffles in battles of strength. Stringing together words and indicating singularity, plurality, time, place and emotion again became a far more streamlined way of communicating, far more effective and capable of needed complexity non-verbal communication could never accomplish. Yet it was the non-verbal language of hunting, maternal sustenance and ultimately farming that filtered into the modern day institution of sports.

The crouch has obvious links to reaching for the soil or an object to be scooped up but it is a key posture in the hunt to avoid visualization by the opponent whether human or animal; in sports ,crouching is quite common in American football in order to lower one's center of gravity while running thus making tackling more difficult; there is also crouching in tennis while at the net to allow for more strategic strikes and in golf where short shots benefit from proximity the striker assumes before hitting the ball.

As we degenerate physically, stooped posture is the rule. The spine leans forward as dorsiflexion becomes limited due to arthritis in the vertebral column. Additionally, there is the anteropulsion of Parkinson's disease wherein there is the forward flexion as well What would appear to be evident is a kind of recaptured sporting posture, coincidental or otherwise. Movement disorders whether hypo- kinetic (Parkinson's disease) or hyperkinetic (the chorea of Huntington's disease) may also reflect retrogressive links to primitive circuitry constituting brain pathways for movement in sports. Freezing characterizes the motionlessness before putting in golf, the keeping still in the forest while observing the hunted animal and the paucity of movement in Parkinson's disease the most common movement disorder in man.

Crouching was quite au natural in our predecessors, the non-human primates noted here in this image of chimpanzees, neither erect nor bipedal.

Mirror neurons foster modeling. It has been shown that "monkey see monkey do" has clear brain neuron proof via these neurons that activate during copying and learning. We continue in those pathways in medicine via the medical resident directive to his intern in some sacred place called "the hospital"- on a clinical procedure: "See one, do one, teach one". Similarly in sports, it has been found that imitation of the instructor as opposed to some academic understanding of a tennis stroke leads to more success on the court; imprinting is linked to this in lower animal forms such as chickens wherein certain duplicative actions are part of the parent to progeny genetic template. It is learning that is rapid and apparently independent of the consequences of a given behavior.

The Moro reflex induced by startling newborns may have phylogenic roots in our branch grab and subsequent release in astonishment as we fell or jumped out of trees. The Moro reflex begins after briefly allowing a surprised newborn to descend back toward a flat surface as if falling with the arms initially moving away from the body with hands open and ending as is seen on the right with the arms moving back towards the body and the grasp recurring. The stepping reflex (which also can include a startled expression but usually not the crying as is noted in the Moro) may be an infant's recapitulating an instinctive stepping as we proudly landed on both feet after that descent from the trees.

Whether grappling with hunting for prey, clubbing another human in battle or utilizing machine guns for similar purposes, it would seem that the aggression if not murderous violence is part of our nature sparked by our need to survive where food was scarce and enemies abounded. Sports has served to simulate a good deal of this though chariot races and lions den encounters have given way to video sports players/rooters , World Cup competitions and couch potato observation if not devotion.

You can't tell the players without with uniforms; perhaps the uniforms have changed in the major leagues but the mission is the same though metaphorically so: "kill or be killed"; track and field with racing, hurdling, vaulting and javelin throwing have easily understood predecessors on the "playing fields" of Roman legionary warrior or struggling as a wounded gladiator.

If there is a "guiding light" in the primitive world of hunting, perhaps it is a spirit or deity precursor that is honored in this ceremony; the religion of the battle may have required a belief in an overarching caring force amid the encountered danger; the religion that is sports continues the saga as the home run hitter points to the heavens "to give thanks" for the power the Lord granted him to smack the four bagger.

Balance altering movement through jumping and spinning are powerful in sports and its cousin, dance. The brain stem processes the vestibular instability and conveys pleasure to the limbic through such activation

32

No sport speaks more to primal neuroanthropology than boxing, although these bonobos may eventually get into the equally primal wrestling...Well, there is however a World Wrestling Entertainment association...This saga is complicated.

Dementia puglisitica and death can ensue....therein we have some things that would allow instincts to take us down a not so gardenish path...a disastrous wish fulfillment amid potential for the thrill of victory?

The multiplicity of human facial expressions can all be exhibited in the sports arena. The important point on this is that they are emotional system/limbic system generated and largely unconscious. The take home message is not that such expressions would be expected, but that their diverse array would appear to have a needed home in sports where they can represent the evolutionarily derived catharsis not as readily available in "real life".

There may be mild eye drooping here too (ptosis) in the angry outburst exhibited facially. Perhaps Waldo was awoken from sleep. In any case, amygdala activation is likely. Aggressive displays associated with open mouth and teeth display may be revealed too as a player on the ball field arises from some fatigue related strength diminution and strikes back at his opponents.

We've gone to the dogs (and are related).

And we both "dig" sand.

The act of digging was the human archeological forerunner for golf.

Sustenance is provided via the presumed made shot. Can the facial reaction not be akin to some massacre of a predator and then the food reward forthcoming?

It's an open mouthed metaphor.

More "food for thought" re: our genetically linked cousins

Yet our own primal standing and walking is tied in to a treasure trove of brain/mind development not seen in the upright gorilla.

Sports has rudimentary roots. However, the magnitude of the entity, i.e. the entirety of the endeavor, is far from a simple evolutionary spin-off.

A tiger in the rain?.....A team association the animal symbol connotes.

https://en.wikipedia.org/wiki/This_Masquerade

Are we really happy here with this lonely game we play?
Looking for words to say
Searching but not finding, understanding anyway
We're lost in a masquerade

Both afraid to say we're just to far away
From being close together from the start
We tried to talk it over but the words got in the way
We're lost inside this lonely game we play

Thoughts of leaving disappear every time I see your eyes
No matter how hard I try
To understand the reasons why we carry on this way
We're lost in a masquerade

Both afraid to say we're just to far away
From being close together from the start
We tried to talk it over but the words got in the way
We're lost inside this lonely game we play

Thoughts of leaving disappear every time I see your eyes
No matter how hard I try
To understand the reasons why we carry on this way
We're lost in a masquerade
Wohoho, in a masquerade

The anthropomorphized cartoon character Sports God hovers over the field of dreams.

A real field of dreams.......softball and perhaps Little League Baseball.

When exploring these neuroanthropological origins, this issue of consciousness takes on far more critical significance.

It is the contention here that gestures, postures, movements and expressions, so much a part of sports, is critical to what indeed represent the primitive consciousness if not unconsciousness of the sports performer.

Simplistically, we note links to the roots of play, competition, mimicry, chance and vertigo.

Perhaps there is a phylogenic scale of importance here. Earliest would be the vertigo drive previously mentioned. This would be followed by the mimicry basis of sports. Competition would be next on the evolutionary scale. Following that and closest to the modern era would be simulations of original games of chance.

Yet, my hypothesis focuses on what is the unconsciousness of sports, which is most easily appreciated by way of comparing movements that are themselves out of our awareness on the athletic fields.

Tics and Gilles de la Tourette Syndrome (Tourette's) (TS)

Gilles de la Tourette syndrome (Tourette's) is a neurodevelopmental disorder characterized by motor and vocal tics—rapid, repetitive, stereotyped movements or vocalizations.

Spitting, chewing, cursing, repetitive behaviors, rituals, superstitions and stereotypical postures are all features of Tourette's syndrome. It turns out that these are features of activities comprising many team sports, particularly baseball.

This array of movements is characteristic of dysfunction in the orbitofrontal-basal ganglionic circuitry in the brain.

Presumptively, the part of the basal ganglia called the caudate is overactive in Tourette's. "I'm dirty, therefore I must wash" is why there can be obsessive hand washing. An overactive putamen- involved in the generation of automatic movements that can exist as tics is another hyperfunctional zone in this condition.

What remains quite intriguing to neuroscientists is the absence of microscopic neuropathology in Tourette's. It is PET Scan obtained neuroimaging data that supports some kind of aberrant function in these pathways. However, there are no clear chemical or histological abnormalities such as what might be seen in Parkinson's or Alzheimer's disease.

One then must ask why are there absent abnormalities? A reasonable contention is that the definition of Tourette's may be some kind of "retro-condition" rather than a dysfunction on the order of an illness.

Leckman has noted that tic symptoms, the hallmark of TS, may be fragments of innate behavior. As such, the sensory urges that precede tics may illuminate some of the normal internal cues that are intimately involved in the assembly of behavioral sequences. The occurrence of tics in time appears to have fractal characteristics that may help to explain the waxing and waning course of tic disorders.

Thus this author supports the idea that indeed Tourette's is some kind of representation of something built in to us. Indeed, Tourette's becomes problematic to the patient because in some sense "the self" or the individual in society or even alone is under siege by these intruding movements.

Therein lies the sports comparison. The bursts of spitting, the rituals, the chewing, the cursing, and so much a part of "the game behavior" compare favorably to the Tourette tics. And indeed, these actions are likely described as "unconscious" to the player.

According to Como, Obsessive Compulsive Behavior (OCB) is perhaps a more appropriate characterization of this behavioral phenomenon that occurs in TS. Obsessive compulsiveness in TS appears similar to the spectrum of the tic disorder in terms of its onset, severity, and course. As with tics, OCB is typically mild and not always substantially disabling. Although clinical features between TS + OCB and primary Obsessive Compulsive Disorder (OCD) overlap considerably, patients with TS and OCB experience different types of obsessive thoughts and compulsive rituals. The link to sports is apparent. Sports rely on ritualistic behavior, by definition constantly repeated- not only the gestures and expressions described above obviously but also the very acts within the sports that constitute skills- Consider the following: the baseball batter taking twenty five swings before coming to the plate, the outfielder pounding on his glove while waiting for a fly ball, the tennis player or basketball player bouncing the ball ten times before either serving or shooting a foul shot.

Levy has noted that the concept of the repetition compulsion remains an enigma. Its etiology is not fully understood and the purpose it serves continues to be a mystery. Although it is often theorized that the compulsion to repeat may function to facilitate conquering of a past trauma, mastery is rarely achieved. In the Levy article, the concept of the repetition compulsion is reviewed and the unanswered questions that continue to exist about this phenomenon are summarized. A way to conceptualize the compulsion to repeat is then offered. The compulsion to repeat as it specifically relates to the attempt to master a previous trauma is reviewed, followed by an examination of the relationship between the compulsion to repeat and reenactments. Finally, how the compulsion to repeat can be viewed as a post-traumatic stress response and the implications of understanding it in this fashion are then examined.

The derived synthesis? Tourette's and its associated Obsessive Compulsive Behavior represent an attempt to recapture a past trauma so as to mitigate it in the same way that sports is an attempt to recapture the similar experiences perhaps linked to our tribal predator state.

Attention Deficit Hyperactivity Disorder (ADHD)

Bradshaw has pointed out that the frontostriatal system (dorsolateral prefrontal cortex, lateral orbitofrontal cortex, anterior cingulate, supplementary motor area, and associated basal-ganglia structures) is subject to not only Tourette's syndrome but to Attention Deficit Hyperactivity Disorder.

Whereas Tourette's describes some of the content and structure of sports, ADHD speaks to another crucial aspect of athletic participation, again out of conscious awareness-that would be the ability to change focus constantly. The second baseman must be cognizant of the runner leading off first base, the type of swing the batter is using, the number of outs and the score of the game. Multi-tasking is the current description which is very apt here. Again, corollaries to the hunter in the wild with a multitude of threats are suggested.

Attention deficiency is also frequently noted in those with Tourette's syndrome.

Autism

The features noted below are characteristic of Autism. It would be fair to indicate that in many aspects of sports, these same findings are frequently noted:

- Displays indifference
- Prefers sameness, going with the familiar route
- Behaves in bizarre ways
- Does not make eye contact
- Talks incessantly about one topic
- Laughs inappropriately
- Handles or spins objects
- Does not pretend in playing
- Isolative behavior unless forced to join in

There is also the male predominance in so many sports enumerated and a comparable gender tendency in Autism.

Indeed, compartmentalized isolated behavior, arithmetical and spatial skills and preoccupation with hitting targets and abilities in separating figures from background are prototypically male. The echoes of sports participation are there. Baron Cohen has suggested Autism relates to being excessively male.

One might ask are autistic children regressed, prehistoric time traveling "men at war"? An autistic "clueless dissociative state" is often required to succeed in sports (i.e. one "lives" in the sport zone alone). Autistic children have trouble with context issues. The only context in sports or in the military is defeating the enemy. Autistic children have difficulty extracting a large meaning to their activities. For soldiers, such cognition is also contrary to their empathy deficient mission mind set.

Cerebellar and frontal lobe dysfunction characterize Autism. However, similar to the other disorders mentioned, the pathological basis for it is not evident when brains are studied although Gallese suggests that mirror neurons (reflected by mu wave activity in the motor cortex and, part of basic brain circuitry for the internal representation of motor acts), may be dysfunctional in autistic children. A presumed developmental problem exists in Autism and perhaps it is a retrogressive screaming of a primordial brain within the total brain.

Baron Cohen points to the amygdala as particularly problematic in Autism as the disorder is characterized in defects in social behavior wherein the subject has difficulty appreciating another's state of mind.

There is no perfect match for sports here. However, suffice it to say that competitive athletics as opposed to chess is far more about attaining a kind of flow state in performance wherein the opponent is secondary.

Teitelbaum has described pervasive soft movement disorders in infants with Autism in many arenas. No co-existing neurological disease has been tied to such findings in the majority of the autistic patients studied.

One wonders whether this phenomenon relates to some poorly understood clock regression in human evolutionary development.

There is also a spectrum of autistic disorders. Thalidomide with its ability to destroy developing neurons and their branches, impair vasculature in the brain and cut into serotonin release can cause an autistic condition. One wonders however if there is any relevance to thalidomide per se in the etiology of the vast majority of Autism cases in society or as far as unexpected sports links.

Skoyles notes that Autism has been linked to thalidomide exposure at 20-24 days gestation. At this stage, the embryo is roughly the size of this 'C', and has yet to develop its brain (except for brainstem cranial motor nerve nuclei). The neuropathology responsible for Autism is presently unknown, but whatever it is, it may logically be one inducible by such an early occurring brainstem cranial motor nerve nuclei defect. Many mental faculties impaired in autism (such as theory of mind) depend upon the prefrontal cortex. The maturation of cerebral-cerebellar connections due to oddities in axon development is vulnerable to pre-existing brainstem nuclei integrity. Many higher cognitive skills (including prefrontal ones) are dependent upon these links raising the possibility that abnormalities in them might produce Autism. He conjectures that impaired cerebral-cerebellar connections, whether caused early, as by thalidomide, or later (including postnatally) by other factors, is the missing neuropathological cause of Autism.

From the neuroanthropological perspective and linking the vast majority of Autism cases that are not exposed to thalidomide, the individual with Autism may have a kind of independently functioning primitive brain, disconnected to various degrees from the higher cortex.

Recently Treffert has described autistic savants as showing "memory without reckoning" which indicates they typically possess a mechanical ability to reproduce their memories but without meaning or content. He also ties this savant syndrome to the phenomenon of left brain damage and right brain recruitment or compensation. The athlete as mute performer coincides with this model.

Stereotypies In Neurology—
Phylogeny of Neurodegeneration

Stereotypies or repetitive and patterned compulsive behaviors are noted throughout the animal kingdom. The phylogenic link to the human and particularly the human in sports is apparent. A brief overview highlighting stereotypies can be enumerated as follows:

- **Dogs** – grooming behaviors such as licking and self scratching; locomotor behaviors such as running and jumping, pacing, paw shaking, tail swishing and whirling; vocal behaviors such as rhythmic barking or growling; predatory behavior such as staring, air batting, pouncing and fly chasing; sexual behavior such as compulsive mounting.

- **Cats** – similar to dogs with self licking and hair chewing common along with hoarding, wool sucking and pacing

- **Horses** – stall walking, weaving, head bobbing, lip flapping/tonguing, head shaking, masturbation

- **Birds** – feather pulling and skin picking

- **Cows** – tongue and compulsive sucking, weaving, hair licking

- **Bears** – pacing

- **Non-human primates** – hair and skin picking, self sucking, licking and chewing, masturbation and rectal probing, bouncing in place, somersaulting

Stereotyped movements are noted in Autism and even more so in Tourette's. Such movements are critical to this thesis as they speak to spontaneously repetitive functionless and unvarying behaviors noted in sports. Think about the wagging movements of a batter readying to receive a pitch.

Stereotypies can be seen in captive and domesticated animals housed in barren environments. Garner believes that by parallel to human patients, there is a potential psychological distress in animals showing these behaviors.

Sports participation means confronting stress. Hence, there is explanation for stereotypies.

Digging deeper, stereotypies also occur in the epilepsies and are related to temporal lobe seizures where repetitive stereotyped movements are noted during behavioral seizures.

If epilepsy represents a state of altered consciousness with stereotypies, why not consider a similar condition for sports by applying the same construct?

Ictal or seizure related grasping, a variant of stereotypy or an automatic release behavior seen during seizures, is linked to frontal lobe seizures. The primordial branch grasping, the infantile grasping, the weapon/racket grasping all have some commonality. Grasping as a function of the unconscious frontal lobe seizure phenomenology would hardly seem to be a coincidence.

Infantile grasping is also a hallmark of child growth. A demented elderly person will also exhibit a return of the grasp reflex.

When viewed from the perspective of time, human genetic disorders give new insights into our evolution. The X-linked HPRT gene (a defect which causes a deficiency of the enzyme hypoxanthine-guanine phosphoribosyltransferase leading to the Lesch-Nyhan syndrome of which the hallmark is self-mutilation) is unique to human, chimpanzee, and gorilla. Stereotypic movements in the face (orofacial dyskinesias seen almost as ritualistic in baseball players on the field), and limbs (fencing posture, as if ready to strike) in addition to coprolalia (also seen in baseball commonly) are characteristic of the Lesch-Nyhan afflicted boys. Orofacial dyskinesias, self injurious behavior and stereotypies are also noted in other genetic neurodegenerative disorder such as Chorea-Acanthocytosis, Huntington's disease and the aforementioned Tourette's syndrome.

Parent provides an overview of the phylogenic evolution and structural organization of the basal ganglia linked to stereotypical movements in addition to violent behavior such as self-mutilation. These large subcortical structures that form the core of the cerebral hemispheres directly participate in the control of psychomotor behavior. Neuroanatomical methods combined with transmitter localization procedures were used to study the chemical organization of the forebrain in each major group of vertebrates. The various components of the basal ganglia appear well developed in amniote vertebrates, but remain rudimentary in anamniote vertebrates. For example, a typical substantia nigra composed of numerous dopaminergic neurons that project to the striatum already exists in the brain of reptiles. Other studies in mammals show that glutamatergic cortical inputs establish distinct functional territories within the basal ganglia; those neurons in each of these territories act upon other brain neuronal systems principally via a GABAergic disinhibitory output mechanism. The functional status of the various basal ganglia chemospecific systems was examined in animal models of neurodegenerative diseases, as well as in postmortem material from Parkinson's and Huntington's disease patients. The neurodegenerative processes at play in such conditions specifically target the most phylogenically ancient components of the brain, including the substantia nigra and the striatum, and the marked involution of these brain structures is accompanied by severe motor and cognitive deficits. Studies of neural mechanisms involved in these akinetic and hyperkinetic disorders have led to a complete reevaluation of the current model of the functional organization of the basal ganglia in both health and disease.

So we evolve, we grow, we involute, we exhibit these phenomena that link all these processes. The basal ganglia contains this primordial motor circuitry that reveals an ancient phylogeny.

And with sports, in adopting the exaggerated movements of certain genetic and neurodegenerative diseases, the Lesch-Nyhanesque self injurious actions of the star shooting guard, the freezing in Parkinson's to steady the tourney winning golfer before a winning putt, or the involuntary dance like movement of Huntington's simulated by the jittery running back eluding a tackler, we are doing a replay of many of these basal ganglia mediated gestures, postures, habits, and behavioral actions, as unconsciously as have been the very evolutionary, ontological and involutionary processes such movements reflect.

Memory-Explicit and Implicit;
The Complex Motor Programs

Declarative and nondeclarative memory constitute active memory systems in man.

In declarative or explicit memory, facts or events are consciously recalled and stored in the medial temporal lobe.

Explicit recall of our pre-historic savagery may have been a non-starter in the development of sports. There may have been too much suppression of id like activity so integral to sports.

On the contrary, nondeclarative or implicit memory is unconscious, evident by way of procedural skills and habits, simple classical conditioning and nonassociative learning. The part of the basal ganglia called the striatum is involved in procedural skills, the amygdala and cerebellum are key to classical conditioning models (for example- learning to move away in a coordinated fashion from a fear engendering object) and reflex pathways such as the ability to land correctly from a biomechanical standpoint is characteristic of nonassociative learning.

When experimental psychologists speak of nonassociative learning, they are referring to those instances in which an animal's behavior toward a stimulus changes in the absence of any apparent associated stimulus or event (such as a reward or punishment). Studies have identified two major forms of simple nonassociative learning, which are to some extent mirror images of one another: habituation and sensitization.

Nonassociative learning is a behavioral change brought on by repeated presentation of one stimulus. In the case of sensitization, a stimulus that originally elicited a weak or non-response starts evoking stronger responses after several presentations, or when the presentation of one very intense stimulus evokes stronger responses to other stimuli. For example, after a very loud crash sound, smaller noises can startle a person, which otherwise would go almost unnoticed. In the case of habituation, repeated presentation of the same stimulus produces decreasing responses to it. In the example of the loud crash, if it keeps sounding repeatedly every twenty seconds, the startle to it will decrease in further presentations.

All of these nondeclarative memory systems involve a perceptomotor skill learning. The problem is the word learning implies an acquired ability. Given so much evolutionary similarity in certain movements, one wonders how much is truly learned as opposed to representing hard-wired program activation.

Pearson has delineated vertebrate motor systems in

which stimulation of either localized regions in the Central Nervous System (CNS) or single interneurons evoke coordinated motor activity. On the list are walking in cat, rats, chicks and birds, swimming in stingrays and turtles, singing in crickets and grasshoppers, escape in fish and crayfish, jumping in flies and flight in locust.

Rhythmic motor systems in which changes are controlled by sensory feedback include chewing in mammals, scratching in the cat and walking in stick insects.

Pearson also describes neuromodulation of pattern generating networks wherein circuits are adapted to behavioral needs as well as establishing the correct configuration of a neuronal circuit for a specific behavior. Most of the neuromodulators are amines and peptides (dopamine, serotonin, glutamate). Calcium and potassium are keys in membrane electrochemistry and in maintaining the long-term depolarization sensitization of learning.

The critical take home point is that this neurophysiological circuitry is on the order of instinct for the animals described, clearly linked to pathways in man.

Dickinson has noted that most pattern neural generators are not isolated and independent entities, producing a relatively defined behavioral pattern or group of behaviors. Instead, they can be dynamic with many neurons shared by the networks that generate more than one behavior.

Warrick echoes these ideas but sites a need to expand vertebrate research.

Pearson indicates that the reason that temporal details of motor patterns are established by afferent feedback is to ensure that the motor pattern is appropriate for the biomechanical state of the motor apparatus.

"Built in posturing" is well described in thinking of a decerebrate cat dropped a few feet to land in a biomechanically advantageous posture.

Katz has noted how motor patterns are initiated and altered on a moment-to-moment basis to suit the needs of the animal. He makes the point that we need a paradigm shift regarding such control of motor circuits, similar to the shift that has already occurred in our understanding of the pattern-generating circuits themselves. Such flexibility of control is the basis for decision making in the nervous system and the very essence of what animals must do throughout their daily lives.

All of this relates to a few critical issues neuroanthropologically:

1. Animals have neural circuitry that is both innate, evolutionarily based and able to show some plasticity depending on the situation
2. Some of these pathways are active in similar patterns across a phylogenic array of animals from invertebrates to mammals
3. More corollaries to the human animal need to be made
4. There is a crucial role for all of this in the neuroanthropology of sports

If we assume that the circuitry so described is active in our implicit memory it is quite rational to apply the implicit memory board of the human- the basal ganglia system to our understanding. It is reasonable to speak of inherited hardware that evolved, as per Hikoska, to accomplish the goal of preventing the explosion of chaotic neural signals and select signals appropriate for the current behavioral context. Again, this is accomplished unconsciously when one is riding a bicycle or running the high hurdles. The implication is the entire sports domain is under such unconscious directives.

Dopamine is key in the basal ganglia and limbic system operation. Hikosaka goes on to note that the procedural memories thus created in the subcortex and overlying hemisphere, particularly premotor cortices, are then used to guide learning of individual movements in which the cerebellum plays a crucial role.

Jueptner notes the neocerebellum (not the basal ganglia) is involved in 1) monitoring and 2) optimizing movements using sensory (proprioceptive) feedback. Thirdly, the relative contribution of sensory information processing to the signal during active/passive execution of a motor task (flexion and extension of the elbow) was examined; it was found that 80-90% of the neocerebellar signal could be attributed to sensory information processing. The basal ganglia were not involved in sensory information processing. That region may be concerned with movement/ muscle selection (efferent motor component); the neocerebellum may be concerned with monitoring the outcome (afferent sensory component) and optimizing movements using sensory (feedback) information.

The procedural non-declarative memory of sports actions thus involves the basal ganglia circuitry plus the refining and coordinating of movements via the cerebellum. These systems are quite independent of the complex declarative memory system that is so crucial to more recent cortical evolution in man, having to do with language.

Abes alludes to many issues of implicit and explicit learning in another way in his comparison of tennis players serving with external and internal attentional focus. Players who have an external focus, i.e. those not attentive to the mechanics of their serving motion and purveying the match situation itself (opponent, the score, the weather), do worse than those who serve without hyperanalysis of their own movements. One could say that they rely on implicit learning and simply non-declarative memory to be successful in sports actions.

Psychoanalysis and the Neurosocial Anthropology of Sports

It is crucial to remember that there is brain circuitry and mind circuitry. If we are no more than somewhat more complicated monkeys, could psychoanalysis have emerged?

When Joe Namath and his band of players, in one way banished from the National Football League to perform in a renegade outfit like the American Football League, played in Super Bowl lll in 1969 in the Orange Bowl in Miami, they were on a grand sports stage of the psyche.

Don Shula, the opposing coach of the National Football League Baltimore Colts, was the father figure that the Oedipal Namath had to kill. As Heim has noted in the analysis of Freud's *Totem and Taboo*, "patricide and the advent of a fatherless society promises emancipation from mythic forces".

With the "murder" of Shula, and the liberation of the taboo American Football League (AFL), players in this new league became famous for "emancipated" play, wide open offense and against the grain strategies of big plays. Heim however went on to indicate that after the patricide, "latent guilt ensures that those mythic forces remain operative and periodically explode into murderous activity". The overall myth of pro football continued but "murderous activity" was noted when AFL player Jack Tatum struck another AFL player, Daryl Stingley so hard in the neck, he was turned into a quadriplegic.

Namath in turn became a playboy which in some psychiatric circles implies the Oedipal marriage to his mother.

"Mythic forces" continued to be operative through the persistent presence of the father, Shula as he returned to join the renegades and then take the American Football League Miami Dolphins to a perfect season. This is again consistent with the Freudian view that the patricidal man is ambivalent concerning his act and therefore needed to remove the symbolism of the murdered father by once again elevating the patriarchal figure.

Obviously, the details of this Freudian jaunt are full of speculation as it relates to the Primal Neuroanthropology of Sports. But thematically, there is a corollary with what has been cited in the neurological and the motor learning domain. Sports are an internalized re-enactment of primal psychic drama.

Sports are a Freudian totem, the deity reigning over the society, representing a super-idol, with specialized actors, animals-natural forces and forms. In effect, it is the ultimate Jungian symbol of a collective unconscious. Yankees, Mets,

Indians, Braves, Pirates, Raiders, Patriots, Buccaneers, 76'ers, combine with Dolphins, Lions, Tigers, Bruins, Marlins and Heat, Lightning, Magic and North Stars.

Freud stressed how magic served a neurotic function. Magic Johnson might have done the same by reaching near deity status as a player of supernatural abilities and then attaining even more grandiose status when he proclaimed his oneness with this subjects through his victimhood as an AIDS patient, only to go on to appear to defeat the human illness.

In a similar way, sports figures serve as deities for the society. On the court, Dwyane Wade, Lebron, Embiid and Leonard perform magical cures for the mundane life of their fans.

The ritual preoccupation instilled in the young to "be like Mike" (Jordan) follows this trend to turn sports into a religion, where emulation of the deity is honored. Of course, Freud may have added to the confusion. Jordan had a conflictual relationship with his father who was murdered by those involved in the world of gambling Jordan had sinfully entered.

Heim reflects on the recurrent failure of culture, its constant relapse into murder and barbarism and sees this in connection with the dialectic nature of enlightenment, the patently intrinsic ambiguity of all progress achieved by Homo sapiens.

Morality, genetic proclivity, violence, and the sadomasochism of sports merge on the playing field as they did in the Iraq War or in the movie 300. There is intrinsic sadomasochism in football. Indeed, there is man on man violence. Men tackling other men in a bedroom might be part of a homosexual act. Tim Hardaway, the former professional basketball star, recently emoted over his hatred of gays and admitted to homophobia. But is not the entire sports team member bonding in some way linked to a homosexual merging?

Morality is a specifically human construct, but does it represent a pronouncement against latent feelings so evident when packs of men function as one? Hence, there is much consternation about gays in the military, another violent theatre that is male dominated.

And so many professional basketball players on the women's side are lesbians. Is the lesbian in pro basketball exhibiting the Electra complex whereby she attempts to bond with the father by assuming his sports behavior, thus killing the mother and her femininity? It seems striking how male homosexuality in basketball is not more blatant-it speaks to societal taboos or as Muscarella has suggested, sexuality too complex to be described by one simple model or a single research discipline.

But to return to the unconscious, the famous anthropologist Malinowski who studied New Guinea tribes in the early 1900's by participating in their society made these stunning observations:

> Yet it must be remembered that what appears to us an extensive, complicated, and yet well ordered institution is the outcome of so many doings and pursuits, carried on by savages, who have no laws or aims or charters definitively laid down. They have no knowledge of the total outline of any of their social structure. They know their own motives, know the purpose of individual actions and the rules which apply to them, but how, out of these, the whole collective institution shapes, this is beyond their mental range. Not even the most intelligent native has any clear idea of the Kula as a big, organized social construction, still less of its sociological function and implications.

This speaks to the unconsciousness of sports in general. We are aware of the athlete's individual motives and the larger structure of games and leagues. However, we have missed the Total Outline of the neurological, psychosocial and evolutionary construction described above in the numerous unconscious actions of those participating in athletics.

Psychopathy, Psychosis, Dreams and More Neurodegeneration—The Sports Connection

Freud focused on the neurotic. Indeed, the roots of sports speak to neurotic behavior and its primal derivation.

But given the multidisciplinary conceptualization, psychosis cannot be ignored.

Buckholtz has recently defined psychopaths, i.e. those exhibiting antisocial behavior, sensation seeking and impulsive behavior, to have an overactive dopamine reward circuit at the level of the nucleus accumbens (which along with the olfactory turbercle forms the ventral striatum) that may lead them to pay more attention to obtaining rewards at the cost of attending to other things such as the potential consequences of their actions to their victims or themselves.

Such a "devil may care" *modus operandus* would appear to reflect the "win at all costs" theme among professional athletes. Death from steroids might be ignored. Brain damage via repeated concussions might be minimized. Lack of empathy for one's opponent, also characteristic of psychopaths, is almost a requirement on the athletic fields.

There is a fascinating theory of human evolution based on the activity of the hunter. Rosse has described how the human primate evolved psychosis generating brain mechanisms in the service of certain feeding behaviors (appetite, foraging) during the course of evolution. These psychosis generating mechanisms may have grown directly out of brain mechanisms servicing appetite. He links this theory to Neuropeptide Y (NPY) which has psychomimietic effects that might have helped in obtaining food resources in stressful environments which were food resource rich but competitor dangerous. Intriguingly, cigarette smoke and perhaps burning leaves in the forest enhance NPY activity while shutting down appetite. NPY may have provided feelings to the hunter of decreased anxiety, decreased fatigability and perhaps grandiose delusions of physical ability and supernatural support.

Linkage of Schizophrenia and sports can thus be formulated. The athlete is the lean mean fighting machine, narcissistic in his powers of movement and strength displayed before the worshipping throngs in the smoke filled stadium, delusional in his belief in the supernatural embrace by the sports god he points to after striking a game winning hit while the mythic competitors so named after animals or warriors engage him in battle. He hears the fans' chants, those command hallucinations to perform or be banished, the way he "heard" the gods direct him against all odds in the jungle.

Nearly 182 years ago, Darwin gave his first speech on

evolution. Crow posits that this was the day Schizophrenia became understood as an evolutionary disease of the brain-the price we pay for developing language.

Crow believes that Schizophrenia is a purely genetic condition that arises as a component of the variation generated in the speciation of Homo sapiens through the evolution of the faculty of language. A critical genetic change on the X and Y chromosomes allowed the two hemispheres to develop with a degree of independence.

Where is the link to sports? Sports is largely mute; it is thus a right hemispheric disconnection phenomenon, highly spatial, and highly independent of language.

Certain positive features of Schizophrenia, i.e. impulsiveness, confabulation, grandiosity, increased sexuality, and mania are associated with right frontal aspects of Schizophrenia and have applications to sports.

This is a highly general construct and will be elaborated upon at close in the context of other neuropsychiatric disorders already mentioned.

The larger point however is that sports represents a psychotic activity, for both the participant and the viewer. Mania, a psychotic feature by itself, need not be part of Schizophrenia, but is quite often seen in its presentation. Mania may have links to the flow state earlier mentioned. It is a kind of other world mindset that allows the player to lose himself or herself in the activity completely through the attainment of a behavioral frenzy.

Are dreams an "acceptable" psychosis the way sports is? One needs look at the helter skelter content of so many dreams and the lack of clear meaning to conjure up ties to a psychotic state in wakefulness.

Given the isolated construct that is sports, why is sports participation and viewing not a waking dream?

If we return to the primal nature of the thalamo-brain stem-occipital cortex dream generators, a number of fascinating relationships to sports and psychosis are apparent:

1. Gardner has described frequently noted fine limb movements associated with awakenings from Rapid Eye Movement/Dream sleep. Perhaps there is a link to some "automatic behavior" in sports.

2. Vertrugno has noted that in the neurodegenerative disorder Multi- System Atrophy wherein primitive parts of the brain are shrunken, there are vocal derangements that mimic ape like stridorous sounds. (quite common during match play among tennis professionals).

3. Fantini has noted that dreams in patients with REM sleep behavior disorder (in which elderly men typically "act out dreams") were characterized by an elevated proportion of aggressive contents, despite normal levels of daytime aggressiveness. Dreams with aggressiveness and the known excessive phasic muscle activity during REM sleep may be related to the hyperactivity of a common neuronal generator. Here is further evidence for violence built into our unconsciousness through its elaboration via "waking dreams". Sports is another frequently violent activity constructed through the assemblage of unconscious movement and behavior.

4. Parkinson's disease, parkinsonian disorders, Diffuse Lewy Body disease, Alzheimer's disease and the frontotemporal dementias are frequently associated with primitive molecules in the brain (synuclein or tau) and disturbed dream sleep. Hallucinations are quite common in the parkinsonian and Diffuse Lewy Body disorders, often with violent thrashing or more complex behavioral actions. Evolutionary retrogression is suggested, the kind that forms the sports primal neuroanthropological thesis.

Sport by Sport Compared One by One; General Conclusions

Summarizing the Primal Neuroanthropology of Sports is a daunting task. Here are models of some major sports and their evolutionary roots:

- **Swimming:** Invertebrate motor system via stimulation of single interneurons
- **Cycling, Track, Gymnastics:** High velocity and "Balance Altering Movement" to attain the speed rush flow state or the whirling dervish high
- **Basketball:** hanging and leaping in trees, reaching for fruit, sometimes very delicately from long range
- **Soccer:** running in open fields either being chased or chasing food
- **Tennis:** bursting through jungle with primitive tools to slash through brush and/or kill animals
- **Boxing and Wrestling:** Perfecting the art of directly destroying animals and humans
- **Baseball:** Long-distance killing and the use of powerful killing tools, unique time perceptions
- **Golf and Hockey:** Cultivating agriculture, tilling the soil, advanced use of driving weaponry
- **Football:** Direct more sophisticated combat with human enemy- use of armor- more intricate patterns of throwing, running, kicking and mass killing

These evolutionary links are of course only a component of the sports origin puzzle. Common principles of motor control in vertebrates and invertebrates have been described. Motor programs and central pattern generators across the animal kingdom clearly indicated basic movements from swimming to chewing to posturing to jumping so integral to sports gestures and motions.

What is certain is that so many of these movements, expressions, and positions are performed unconsciously and have ties to infantile stances or involutional reflexes in the elderly.

Stereotyped and preservative behavior characterizes so much of the performance routine in sporting matches. Ridley notes that repetitive behavior is also a feature of neuropsychiatric conditions including Schizophrenia, Autism, OCD, Addictive Disorders, some neurological disorders including frontal lobe lesions, Tourette's syndrome and PD.

Tourette's has multiple ties to the various rituals in baseball, whether it is the cursing, spitting or tic like repetitions with hand to baseball glove.

The Free Safety in football, able to participate in numerous varying activities on the field depending upon the play, suggests the lateralized thinking of the creative mind, a creativity that may be unleashed in certain neurodegenerative disorders of the brain such as the fronto-temporal dementias.

Variability in tasking is characteristic of the rapid shifting mind of the child with Attention Deficit Hyperactivity Disorder. Such a condition would apply to so many players in a diverse array of team sports, if not individual sports where changing reactions based on awareness of differing simultaneously received stimuli are typical.Replaying post-traumatic stress according to many can have an analgesic effect. Are sports exemplary of a regression to mitigate an acquired trait of hunting memory? Certainly the procedural memory rather than the declarative memory intrinsic to sports and perhaps other organized violent activities such as war may be operational.

Cooing, lip smacking, teeth displays seen on fields of play are not learned. They are innate and noted in our monkey and ape ancestors. From whence came "the chain pull" in response to a victorious shot? We affirm our pre-descent tree branch grasp in this flexed motion of triumph! The cricket swing, the racquetball backhand, the ring toss motion, the serve, the overhand pitch, the delicate jump shot, the volleyball tap to a team member all can generate analogies to the food gathering and hunting activity of primitive man. The function of play, dance, games and sports speaks to either a rehearsal of work, a mockery of mundane activity, a re-enactment of some primal sequence or all of the above. The calculations and compulsive statistical compilation in sports must add up to something outside of accounting for accounting's sake. Sports is a business, but it is a business of men playing children's games—games with no direct application to the larger functioning of the work world. Sports might be assuaging something, beyond its obvious general escape value.

And sports may contain a psychic aberrancy beyond a primal replay. Crawford notes: A greater understanding of psychopathology will be found in the integration of genetic and evolutionary perspectives on adaptation and function. Evolutionary theory proposes that adaptive traits are reproduced more successfully than maladaptive ones. However, some traits, while contributing to fitness in the ancestral environment, may contribute to fitness no longer. This is known as mismatch theory. Sports in this way may be an extension of Schizophrenia and represent such a vestigial psychopathy, since so much of this condition cannot lead to successful application within the culture.

But in the tragedy of life, in the inexplicability of day to day actions, in the mundaneness of not being psychotic, who is to say that Schizophrenia is not a reasonable escape, available to only a few. And perhaps the organized psychosis that is sports represents what civilization will allow— running amok but within the confines of scorekeeping and superego imposed rules. In modern life, replete with defense mechanisms and neuroses, do we need an escape from our savage self? Such was the Freudian thesis, as Oedipus solves the riddle of the totemic sphinx but in the process loses cognizance of his primal nature. Is sports representative of an unconscious playing out of the hunting Cro-Magnon that lies within us?

Namath murdered the father, Shula. Long live sports!

Late Breaking Issues—
More On Sports, The Self and Consciousness

Theories of consciousness have inserted themselves into the world of Neurology as much as they have been mainstays in Psychology, Psychiatry and to a degree Social Anthropology. Suffice it to say that no clear localization of consciousness has been found. On the contrary, consciousness is increasingly realized to be a multi-dimensional construct, that is to say consciousness is not "one thing", just as "the self" may also not represent one abstract entity.

Theory of mind revolves around the innate ability of humans and perhaps non-human primates to have some appreciation of the state of mind of others. Evidence for this would appear to come from the discovery of mirror neurons in the latter group and the implication that they exist frontally in humans. Infants would appear to have a nascent understanding of some mental states in others as do chimpanzees.

Ferrari has found that the macaque "has access to others minds" through gaze. This has been proposed to be a precursor for more complex cognitive skills related to mind reading.

What is evident here is that "the reading" of one's opponent on the playing field is a kind of basic ability for the sports competitor. There is also the issue of learning fundamental actions such as sports swings through modeling. These ideas would appear to have these genetic links installed within our neuroanatomy in the frontal and prefrontal cortices.

The consciousness link here is that there is a kind of "pre-reflective" consciousness (a term used by Legrand) in operation with such activity which can be applied to the athletic world. A pre-reflective consciousness circuitry may well have been identified by Boly and Owen who found that patients studied by fMRI in a vegetative state activated their supplemental motor area (SMA) in the pre-frontal cortex when told to "play tennis" as opposed to the parietal regions in spatial navigation through a home they were told to imagine. The rich links to the basal ganglia from the SMA speaks to activation of this fundamental motor program.

Their work has been ballyhooed as a new understanding of the vegetative state and of course it also speaks to varying realms of consciousness. There is of course a tie-in with some of the psycho- philsosophical constructs in the consciousness arena as related to our understanding of the brain/mind of man and such application to sports. Tsakiris has made the distinction between a sense of agency and a sense of body ownership as distinctly different forms of consciousness.

Synofzik has expanded on this in his conceptualization of "the acting self", a kind of efferent self as opposed to the self who owns, one who possesses through afferent stimuli various body parts. Concepts of the alien hand, the anarchic hand and anosagnosia for one's hemiparesis would fall into the category of the latter. Phantom limb issues may apply to both constructs but can clearly be noted in the motor cortex activation corresponding to the region in either hemisphere that no longer has a limb to carry out its commands.

Gallese has advanced a fusion of ideas whereby he speaks of a primitive sense of self wherein the body is primarily given to us as a source of power for action, not only for movements and behaviors in our environment but in interactions with other bodies (with mirror neuron mechanisms underpinning key aspects by reflecting an internal motor description of the perceived motor act's goal).

This thesis coincides with the sports self, as opposed to the introspective if not ruminating self-reflective self and is linked to the Knox synthesis that the development of archetypes relates to "embodied simulation" via the pan-humankind inhibition of the connections between secondary pre-motor cortical areas and the primary motor cortex (coincident with the Gallese-Lakoff hypothesis that at least one level of abstract thought is a form of simulated action- though there are many issues of simulation that need clarification in that, as per Lyons, non-human primates have plenty of mirror neurons frontally and parietally don't imitate well- perhaps they still have intentional understanding). One might say that archetypal postures, movements, behaviors, league/team structure lay the foundation for sports activity but not a superseding awareness of the existence of same archetypal components. "Being like Michael Jordan" (as per the aforementioned Nike campaign to encourage sneaker buyers to "graduate to a higher level of being") and expanding that attempted imitation to great numbers of children does not mean that same Michael Jordan basketball stylistics are appreciated as representing larger principles to the masses of replicators or those who advertise to them.

Rather, the Jordan campaign may reflect the Malinowski idea that society has institutions that are perceived without introspection over their greater meaning. Such yearnings to emulate god-like figures serve only as vehicles for self satisfaction. This ideation points to the sports self as effectively part of mankind's anosagnosia. One can imitate a mentor in tennis. One can spread the acquired knowledge extracted from observing athletic movements via coaching and book writing on technique. However, the core reason for same activities may escape same protagonists, perpetrating the institutionalized obliviousness to a visceral understanding of sports.

Povinelli has written about "what young chimpanzees know about seeing". Answer- not much. Likewise, we carry that kind of void in our sports minds. It's part of our primitive genetic memory.

Samsonovich posits the self as the subject of experience in contrast to a state of self-awareness, a body image or a narrative center. He speaks eerily of "the main player" not being consciousness *per se* but its subject.

All of this points to the human typified by a tunnel visioned athletic team member/stadium ticket holding state as this more generalizable "main player" (perhaps represented by Treffert's autistic savant who has a defective higher cortico-limbic circuit for semantic and cognitive memory and compensation by the lower level cortico-striatal circuit for the more primitive habit memory). This player is functional for reward seeking purposes in games/sports and an unconscious participant in societal lynchpins, again to self satisfy. Duke University Coach Mike Krzyzewski (Coach K) forgot to acknowledge his wife at courtside after a big win. This life partner effectively didn't exist amid the narrow magic of the on court victory thrill.

We function as if football and other sports are givens in nature, like the beach, the hills, and the trees. The invention of sports, games, Olympic competition and the organization of such activity somehow absents a kind of awareness of their man made creation. Were they discovered as if unearthed dinosaurs? Were James Naismith and Abner Doubleday archeologists?

The fundamental consciousness that's both part of sports fanaticism and the athletes' on field behavior/movements is an arena requiring ongoing research as it reflects our overall Primal Neuroanthropology and our Primal Neuroanthropology of Sports.

Post-Script

We note in the recent articles whose URL's are listed below that prehistoric man lives on through violence. The critical question for our civilization now is what can we do about it? In the name of sport, a boxer Maxim Dadashev, in the past few days, was killed due to blows to the head during a match. **https://www.nytimes.com/2019/07/23/sports/maxim-dadashev-dead-boxer.html**

In another report, a Mixed Martial Arts (MMA) fighter sustained the kind of horrific skull fracture reported during tribal and perhaps family violence unearthed 7000 and and then 3000 years ago (see URL below MMA reference).

MMA: **https://www.cbssports.com/mma/news/mma-fighter-suffers-fractured-skull-after-catching-flying-knee-in-ko-loss/**

Tribal Violence: **https://www.newscientist.com/article/dn28056-shattered-stone-age-bones-expose-worlds-oldest-mass-torture/**

If we have a "Primal Neuroanthropology (PNA) of Sports" that lives on, it speaks to numerous drives and behaviors elaborated upon in this book.

However, PNA also reflects great danger to our species hiding under plain sight in the form of sports violence that in one way or the other, though addressed through new rules and regulations, continues to plague the institution of sports.

Yes, one can be run over by a car via an accident while crossing the street as a pedestrian. Accidents can happen. Accidents can occur in the ring or on the gridiron. The difference, however, is that an automobile tragedy is generally not a function of a perceived risk. It is an extremely rare unwanted occurrence in a situation dedicated to security. In violent sports, particularly in sports involving head trauma, the risk is built in to an acceptance of the sports itself.

Death can therefore be interpreted as a type of dare devil rolling of the dice by the participants where brain injury can induce Chronic Traumatic Encephalopathy (CTE) most commonly described now in professional football players over age 40, what has been called dementia pugilistica historically in boxers and through the outrageous situations described via the URL's of the articles listed on this page. In part outrageous because boxing induced brain swelling and death a few days later is one disaster and an MMA induced skull fracture where the brain sequelae are not well articulated in the lay press is a second idiocy.

The latter point, wherein potential brain injury is sidestepped in reporting, deserves expounding upon as there is a great tendency to understate injury in sport or to constantly refer to "complete recoveries" when none have really occurred. Until recognized in recent years with the delineation of CTE, repetitive head injury had been minimized or not fully investigated. Dr. Bennet Omalu shed new light on the subject by way of identifying traumatic brain lesions to be associated with the deaths of Pittsburgh Steeler players who developed behavioral and cognitive disturbances in mid life. **http://www.protectthebrain.org/ Our-Team/Bennet-I-Omalu-M-D-.aspx**

However, Maxim Dadashev died just within the past week as if acute manifestations of head injury such as the subdural hematoma and cerebral edema he sustained in the ring are simply bad luck because over 99 percent of bouts in the ring don't end in death. I believe no sport is acceptable with this kind of risk or even non-fatal cognitive degeneration that is a rampant problem the more football players, boxers, MMA participants and wrestlers are investigated. Rapid or slow onset suicide might be acceptable if we ruminate about it long enough but why allow such "logic" into the world of sports?

The "why" is an underpinning of this book.

As noted in another story on Stone Age discoveries, **https://www.newscientist.com/article/2208455- modern-forensics-solves-stone-age-murder-mystery- after-33000-years/**, humans have been engaged in murder- ous whacking of the skulls of other humans for millennia. Bats are often the tools of choice and such a selection would appear to spill over into the many sports involving striking with such instruments. The neutralizing of an opponent via a bat attack to the cranium or the utilization of an extremity to strike the blow in one to one scenarios would appear to be in our genetic program.

In considering all the enjoyment derived from sports and the vast amount of time no acute serious injury is sustained, the question emanates: How much violence is mankind willing to accept particularly in view of acute and chronic sequelae of brain injury?

We must look hard at the species to answer that. It's impossible to do so comprehensively in one initial book on *Primal Neuroanthropology a NeuroSports Hypothesis*, but I believe we should demand this "second look operation" on sports (including a follow-up tome coming soon called *Primal Sports II: A Psychoanalytical, Neurosociological, New Games, Myth and Satire Laden Treatise).*

Sports is not oxygen.

Sports is not gravity.

Sports is not a law of physics. On the other hand, it has been treated as such mostly because it involves rewards and tendencies that cannot easily be shut down thereby evolving into the axiomatic.

Thrill seeking is ingrained. Death, injury and disability are inevitable. Thus, we have justification galore for unfortunate outcomes in athletes.

Why we play, why we are athletes and why we invented sports are important associated questions in better appreciating who we were , who we are and who we will become.

******

Bibliography

Abes L, Takase, E Attentional Strategy and Tennis Serve Performance in ITF Coaching (Brazil) May 28, 2007.

Alford S, Schwartz E, Viana di Prisco G. The pharmacology of vertebrate spinal central pattern generators. Neuroscientist. 2003 Jun;9(3):217-28. Review. PubMed PMID: 15065817.

Amaral DG, Bauman MD, Schumann CM. The amygdala and autism: implications from non-human primate studies. Genes Brain Behav. 2003 Oct;2(5):295-302. Review. PubMed PMID: 14606694.

Ames D, Cummings JL, Wirshing WC, Quinn B, Mahler M. Repetitive and compulsive behavior in frontal lobe degenerations. J Neuropsychiatry Clin Neurosci. 1994 Spring;6(2):100-13. Review. PubMed PMID: 8044031.

Anandan S, Wigg CL, Thomas CR, Coffey B. Psychosurgery for self-injurious behavior in Tourette's disorder. J Child Adolesc Psychopharmacol. 2004 Winter;14(4):531-8. Review. PubMed PMID: 15662144.

Anderson JR, Myowa-Yamakoshi M, Matsuzawa T. Contagious yawning in chimpanzees. Proc Biol Sci. 2004 Dec 7;271 Suppl 6:S468-70. PubMed PMID: 15801606; PubMed Central PMCID: PMC1810104.7

Anderson KN, Smith IE, Shneerson JM. Rhythmic movement disorder (head banging) in an adult during rapid eye movement sleep. Mov Disord. 2006 Jun;21(6):866-7. PubMed PMID: 16541454.

Andrews PW, Gangestad SW, Matthews D. Adaptationism--how to carry out an exaptationist program. Behav Brain Sci. 2002 Aug;25(4):489-504; discussion 504-53. Review. PubMed PMID: 12879701.

Angelaki DE. Eyes on target: what neurons must do for the vestibuloocular reflex during linear motion. J Neurophysiol. 2004 Jul;92(1):20-35. Review. PubMed PMID: 15212435.

Annett M. The theory of an agnosic right shift gene in schizophrenia and autism. Schizophr Res. 1999 Oct 19;39(3):177-82. PubMed PMID: 10507510.

Annett M. Schizophrenia and autism considered as the products of an agnosic right shift gene. Cogn Neuropsychiatry. 1997;2(3):195-214. PubMed PMID: 16571495.

Annett M, Kilshaw D. Mathematical ability and lateral asymmetry. Cortex. 1982 Dec;18(4):547-68. PubMed PMID: 7166042.

Applegate H, Matson JL, Cherry KE. An evaluation of functional variables affecting severe problem behaviors in adults with mental retardation by using the Questions about Behavioral Function Scale (QABF). Res Dev Disabil. 1999 May-Jun;20(3):229-37. PubMed PMID: 10372414.

Arendt T, Bigl V, Arendt A, Tennstedt A. Loss of neurons in the nucleus basalis of Meynert in Alzheimer's disease, paralysis agitans and Korsakoff's Disease. Acta Neuropathol. 1983;61(2):101-8. PubMed PMID: 6637393.

Armstrong E. A comparative review of the primate motor system. J Mot Behav. 1989 Dec;21(4):493-517. PubMed PMID: 15136258.

Armstrong E. Enlarged limbic structures in the human brain: the anterior thalamus and medial mamillary body. Brain Res. 1986 Jan 8;362(2):394-7. PubMed PMID: 3080202.

Atchison PR, Thompson PD, Frackowiak RS, Marsden CD. The syndrome of gait ignition failure: a report of six cases. Mov Disord. 1993 Jul;8(3):285-92. Review. PubMed PMID: 8341292

Augustine LE, Damico JS. Attention deficit hyperactivity disorder: the scopeof the problem. Semin Speech Lang. 1995 Nov;16(4):243-57; quiz 257-8. Review. PubMed PMID: 8574914.

Bachevalier J, Loveland KA. The orbitofrontal-amygdala circuit andself-regulation of social-emotional behavior in autism. Neurosci Biobehav Rev. 2006;30(1):97-117. Epub 2005 Sep 12. Review. PubMed PMID: 16157377.

Baets J, Pals P, Bergmans B, Foncke E, Smets K, Hauman H, Vanderwegen L, Cras P. Opsoclonus-myoclonus syndrome: a clinicopathological confrontation. Acta Neurol Belg. 2006 Sep;106(3):142-6. PubMed PMID: 17091618.21

Baird J, Stevenson JC, Williams DC. The evolution of ADHD: a disorderof communication? Q Rev Biol. 2000 Mar;75(1):17-35. Review. PubMed PMID: 10721532.

Bakchine S, Lacomblez L, Palisson E, Laurent M, Derouesne C. Relationship between primitive reflexes, extra-pyramidal signs, reflective apraxia and severity of cognitive impairment in dementia of the Alzheimer type. Acta Neurol Scand. 1989 Jan;79(1):38-46. PubMed PMID: 2929273.

Barbas H. Anatomic basis of cognitive-emotional interactions in the primate prefrontal cortex. Neurosci Biobehav Rev. 1995 Fall;19(3):499-510. Review.PubMed PMID: 7566750.

Barkley RA. The executive functions and self-regulation: an evolutionary neuropsychological perspective. Neuropsychol Rev. 2001 Mar;11(1):1-29. Review. PubMed PMID: 11392560.25

Baron-Cohen S. Autism: the empathizing-systemizing (E-S) theory. Ann N Y Acad Sci. 2009 Mar;1156:68-80. Review. PMID:1933850326: Barton RA. From The Cover: Binocularity and brain evolution in primates. Proc Natl Acad Sci U S A. 2004 Jul 6;101(27):10113-5. Epub 2004 Jun 15. PubMed PMID: 15199183; PubMed Central PMCID: PMC454173.

Barton RA. How did brains evolve? Nature. 2002 Jan 10;415(6868):134-5. PubMed PMID: 11805823.28

Barton RA, Harvey PH. Mosaic evolution of brain structure in mammals. Nature. 2000 Jun 29;405(6790):1055-8. PubMed PMID: 10890446.

Barton RA. Visual specialization and brain evolution in primates. Proc Biol Sci. 1998 Oct 22;265(1409):1933-7. PubMed PMID: 9821360; PubMedCentral PMCID: PMC1689478.

Bastian AJ, Martin TA, Keating JG, Thach WT. Cerebellar ataxia: abnormal control of interaction torques across multiple joints. J Neurophysiol. 1996 Jul;76(1):492-509. PubMed PMID: 8836239.

Bauman MD, Lavenex P, Mason WA, Capitanio JP, Amaral DG. The development of social behavior following neonatal amygdala lesions in rhesus monkeys. J Cogn Neurosci. 2004 Oct;16(8):1388-411. PubMed PMID: 15509386.

Bemporad JR. Freud, Janet and evolution: of statuettes and plants. J Am Acad Psychoanal. 1989 Winter;17(4):623-38. PubMed PMID: 2621128.

Bengtsson SL, Ehrsson HH, Forssberg H, Ullén F. Effector-independent voluntary timing: behavioural and neuroimaging evidence. Eur J Neurosci. 2005 Dec;22(12):3255-65. PubMed PMID: 16367791.

Berardelli A, Noth J, Thompson PD, Bollen EL, Currà A, Deuschl G, van Dijk JG, Töpper R, Schwarz M, Roos RA. Pathophysiology of chorea and bradykinesia in Huntington's disease. Mov Disord. 1999 May;14(3):398-403. Review. PubMed PMID: 10348461.

Berlim MT, Mattevi BS, Belmonte-de-Abreu P, Crow TJ. The etiology of schizophrenia and the origin of language: overview of a theory. Compr Psychiatry. 2003 Jan-Feb;44(1):7-14. Review. PubMed PMID: 12524630.

Bertrand E, Lechowicz W, Szpak GM, Lewandowska E, Dymecki J, Wierzba-Bobrowicz T. Limbic neuropathology in idiopathic Parkinson's disease with concomitant dementia. Folia Neuropathol. 2004;42(3):141-50. PubMed PMID: 15535032.

Bhatia SC, Manchanda SK, Kapoor BK, Aneja IS. Electrical and chemical stimulation of the same hypothalamic loci in relation to agressive behaviour in cats: a comparison study. Indian J Physiol Pharmacol. 1995 Oct;39(4):369-76. PubMed PMID: 8582749.

Biseul I, Sauleau P, Haegelen C, Trebon P, Drapier D, Raoul S, Drapier S, Lallement F, Rivier I, Lajat Y, Verin M. Fear recognition is impaired by subthalamic nucleus stimulation in Parkinson's disease. Neuropsychologia. 2005;43(7):1054-9. Epub 2004 Dec 30. PubMed PMID: 15769491.

Bloch JI, Boyer DM. Grasping primate origins. Science. 2002 Nov 22;298(5598):1606-10. PubMed PMID: 12446906.

Boecker H, Ceballos-Baumann A, Bartenstein P, Weindl A, Siebner HR, Fassbender T, Munz F, Schwaiger M, Conrad B. Sensory processing in Parkinson's and Huntington's disease: investigations with 3D H(2)(15)O-PET. Brain. 1999 Sep;122 (Pt 9):1651-65. PubMed PMID: 10468505.41.

Boeve BF, Silber MH, Ferman TJ, Lucas JA, Parisi JE. Association of REM sleep behavior disorder and neurodegenerative disease may reflect an underlying synucleinopathy. Mov Disord. 2001 Jul;16(4):622-30. PubMed PMID: 11481685.

Boeve BF, Silber MH, Ferman TJ, Kokmen E, Smith GE, Ivnik RJ, Parisi JE, Olson EJ, Petersen RC. REM sleep behavior disorder and degenerative dementia: an association likely reflecting Lewy body disease. Neurology. 1998 Aug;51(2):363-70. PubMed PMID: 9710004.

Boffelli D, McAuliffe J, Ovcharenko D, Lewis KD, Ovcharenko I, Pachter L, Rubin EM. Phylogenetic shadowing of primate sequences to find functional regions of the human genome. Science. 2003 Feb 28;299(5611):1391-4. PubMed PMID: 12610304.

Bollack J. [The son of man. Freud's Oedipus myth]. Psyche (Stuttg). 1993 Jul;47(7):647-83. German. PubMed PMID: 8362077.

Boly M, Coleman MR, Davis MH, Hampshire A, Bor D, Moonen G, Maquet PA, Pickard JD, Laureys S, Owen AM. When thoughts become action: an fMRI paradigm to study volitional brain activity in non-communicative brain injured patients. Neuroimage. 2007 Jul 1;36(3):979-92. Epub 2007 Mar 13. PubMed PMID: 17509898.

Bouden A, Halayem MB. [Attention deficit and hyperactivity in the child].Tunis Med. 2001 Jun-Jul;79(6-7):335-40. Review. French. PubMed PMID: 11771427.

Braak H, Braak E, Yilmazer D, de Vos RA, Jansen EN, Bohl J. Pattern of brain destruction in Parkinson's and Alzheimer's diseases. J Neural Transm. 1996;103(4):455-90. Review. PubMed PMID: 9617789.

Bracha HS, Bienvenu OJ, Eaton WW. Testing the Paleolithic-human-warfare hypothesis of blood-injection phobia in the Baltimore ECA Follow-up Study--towards a more etiologically-based conceptualization for DSM-V. J Affect Disord. 2007 Jan;97(1-3):1-4. Epub 2006 Jul 24. PubMed PMID: 16860872.

Bracha HS. Human brain evolution and the "Neuroevolutionary Time-depth Principle:" Implications for the Reclassification of fear-circuitry-related traits in DSM-V and for studying resilience to warzone-related posttraumatic stress disorder. Prog Neuropsychopharmacol Biol Psychiatry. 2006 Jul;30(5):827-53. Epub 2006 Mar 23. Review. PubMed PMID: 16563589.

Bracha HS, Yoshioka DT, Masukawa NK, Stockman DJ. Evolution of the human fear-circuitry and acute sociogenic pseudoneurological symptoms: the Neolithic balanced-polymorphism hypothesis. J Affect Disord. 2005 Oct;88(2):119-29.PubMed PMID: 16111764.

Bracha HS, Ralston TC, Williams AE, Yamashita JM, Bracha AS. The clenching-grinding spectrum and fear circuitry disorders: clinical insights from the neuroscience/paleoanthropology interface. CNS Spectr. 2005 Apr;10(4):311-8. Review. PubMed PMID: 15788958.

Bracha HS. Freeze, flight, fight, fright, faint: adaptationist perspectiveson the acute stress response spectrum. CNS Spectr. 2004 Sep;9(9):679-85. Review. PubMed PMID: 15337864.

Bradshaw JL, Sheppard DM. The neurodevelopmental frontostriatal disorders: evolutionary adaptiveness and anomalous lateralization. Brain Lang. 2000 Jun 15;73(2):297-320. Review. PubMed PMID: 10856179.

Bramble DM, Lieberman DE. Endurance running and the evolution of Homo. Nature. 2004 Nov 18;432(7015):345-52. PubMed PMID: 15549097.

Brauth SE. Histochemical strategies in the study of neural evolution. Brain Behav Evol. 1990;36(2-3):100-15. Review. PubMed PMID: 1980223.

Brenner I. On trauma, perversion, and "multiple personality". J Am Psychoanal Assoc. 1996;44(3):785-814. PubMed PMID: 8892188.

Brody JF. Evolutionary recasting: ADHD, mania and its variants. J Affect Disord. 2001 Jul;65(2):197-215. Review. PubMed PMID: 11356245.

Bronstein AM, Hood JD. Oscillopsia of peripheral vestibular origin. Central and cervical compensatory mechanisms. Acta Otolaryngol. 1987 Sep-Oct;104(3-4):307-14. PubMed PMID: 3673562.

Brown S, Martinez MJ, Parsons LM. The neural basis of human dance. Cereb Cortex. 2006 Aug;16(8):1157-67. Epub 2005 Oct 12. PubMed PMID: 16221923.

Brown S. Deterioration. Epilepsia. 2006;47 Suppl 2:19-23. Review. PubMed PMID: 17105454.

Brüne M. Schizophrenia-an evolutionary enigma? Neurosci Biobehav Rev.2004 Mar;28(1):41-53. Review. PubMed PMID: 15036932.62: Bruner E., Jacobs HI Alzheimer's disease: the sdownside of a highly evolved parietal lobe? J Alzheimers Dis 2013; 35: 227-240

Buckholtz JW, Treadway MT, Cowan RL, Woodward ND, Benning SD, Li R,Ansari MS, Baldwin RM, Schwartzman AN, Shelby ES, Smith CE, Cole D, Kessler RM, Zald DH. Mesolimbic dopamine reward system hypersensitivity in individuals with psychopathic traits. Nat Neurosci. 2010 Apr;13(4):419-21. Epub 2010 Mar 14. PubMed PMID: 20228805.

Burgess N, Maguire EA, Spiers HJ, O'Keefe J. A temporoparietal and prefrontal network for retrieving the spatial context of lifelike events. Neuroimage. 2001 Aug;14(2):439-53. PubMed PMID: 11467917.

Byne W, White L, Parella M, Adams R, Harvey PD, Davis KL. Tardivedyskinesia in a chronically institutionalized population of elderly schizophrenic patients: prevalence and association with cognitive impairment. Int J Geriatr Psychiatry. 1998 Jul;13(7):473-9. PubMed PMID: 9695037.

Błaszczyk JW. Motor deficiency in Parkinson's disease. Acta Neurobiol Exp (Wars). 1998;58(1):79-93. Review. PubMed PMID: 9583191.

Cal R, Bahmad Jr F. Vestibular evoked myogenic potentials: an overview. Braz J Otorhinolaryngol. 2009 May-Jun;75(3):456-62. Review. English, Portuguese. PubMed PMID: 19649499.

Callois, R Man, Play and Games,trans. by Barash.   New York, Free Press of Glencoe, 1961.

Calvin, W. H. The throwing madonna: essays on the brain. McGraw-Hill,. New York. 1983

Calvin WH. A stone's throw and its launch window: timing precision and its implications for language and hominid brains. J Theor Biol. 1983 Sep 7;104(1):121-35. PubMed PMID: 6632930.

Camicioli R, Howieson D, Lehman S, Kaye J. Talking while walking: the effect of a dual task in aging and Alzheimer's disease. Neurology. 1997 Apr;48(4):955-8. PubMed PMID: 9109884.

Campos JJ, Thein S, Owen D. A Darwinian legacy to understanding human infancy: emotional expressions as behavior regulators. Ann N Y Acad Sci. 2003 Dec;1000:110-34. PubMed PMID: 14766627.

Cantwell DP. Diagnostic validity of the hyperactive child (attention deficit disorder with hyperactivity) syndrome. Psychiatr Dev. 1983 Autumn;1(3):277-300. Review. PubMed PMID: 6369312.

Carey WB. ADHD as a disorder of adaptation. J Am Acad Child Adolesc Psychiatry. 1998 Aug;37(8):797-8; author reply 798-9. PubMed PMID: 9695438.

Carrey N. ADHD as a disorder of adaptation. J Am Acad Child Adolesc Psychiatry. 1998 Aug;37(8):797; author reply 798-9. PubMed PMID: 969543

Castall B, Marsden CD, Naylor RJ, Pycock CJ. Stereotyped behaviour patterns and hyperactivity induced by amphetamine and apomorphine after discrete 6-hydroxydopamine lesions of extrapyramidal and mesolimbic nuclei. Brain Res. 1977 Mar 4;123(1):89-111. PubMed PMID: 300267.

Castellanos FX, Ritchie GF, Marsh WL, Rapoport JL. DSM-IV stereotypic movement disorder: persistence of stereotypies of infancy in intellectually normal adolescents and adults. J Clin Psychiatry. 1996 Mar;57(3):116-22. PubMed PMID: 8617696.

Cath DC, Spinhoven P, van Woerkom TC, van de Wetering BJ, Hoogduin CA, Landman AD, Roos RA, Rooijmans HG. Gilles de la Tourette's syndrome with and without obsessive-compulsive disorder compared with obsessive-compulsive disorder without tics: which symptoms discriminate? J Nerv Ment Dis. 2001 Apr;189(4):219-28. PubMed PMID: 11339317.

Cath DC, Spinhoven P, van de Wetering BJ, Hoogduin CA, Landman AD, van Woerkom TC, Roos RA, Rooijmans HG. The relationship between types and severity of repetitive behaviors in Gilles de la Tourette's disorder and obsessive-compulsive disorder. J Clin Psychiatry. 2000 Jul;61(7):505-13. PubMed PMID: 10937609.

Cattaneo L, Cucurachi L, Chierici E, Pavesi G. Pathological yawning as a presenting symptom of brain stem ischaemia in two patients. J Neurol Neurosurg Psychiatry. 2006 Jan;77(1):98-100. Epub 2005 Sep 20. PubMed PMID: 16174652; PubMed Central PMCID: PMC2117389.

Ceccherini-Nelli A, Turpin-Crowther K, Crow TJ. Schneider's first rank symptoms and continuous performance disturbance as indices of dysconnectivity of left- and right-hemispheric components of language in schizophrenia. Schizophr Res. 2007 Feb;90(1-3):203-13. Epub 2006 Nov 16. PubMed PMID: 17113266.

Chapman AH, Chapman-Santana M. The influence of Nietzsche on Freud's ideas. Br J Psychiatry. 1995 Feb;166(2):251-3. PubMed PMID: 7728371.

Chasseguet-Smirgel J. Sadomasochism in the perversions: some thoughts on the destruction of reality. J Am Psychoanal Assoc. 1991;39(2):399-415. PubMed PMID: 1856440.

Chaudhari S, Deo B. Neurodevelopmental assessment in the first year with emphasis on evolution of tone. Indian Pediatr. 2006 Jun;43(6):527-34. PubMed PMID: 16820662.

Chemali Z, Meadows ME. The use of eye movement desensitization and reprocessing in the treatment of psychogenic seizures. Epilepsy Behav. 2004 Oct;5(5):784-7. PubMed PMID: 15380136.

Ciompi L. Is there really a schizophrenia? The long-term course of psychotic phenomena. Br J Psychiatry. 1984 Dec;145:636-40. PubMed PMID: 6210125.

Comings DE, Wu S, Chiu C, Ring RH, Gade R, Ahn C, MacMurray JP, Dietz G, Muhleman D. Polygenic inheritance of Tourette syndrome, stuttering, attention deficit hyperactivity, conduct, and oppositional defiant disorder Am J Med Genet. 1996 May 31;67(3):264-88. PubMed PMID: 8725745.

Como PG, LaMarsh J, O'Brien KA. Obsessive-compulsive disorder in Tourette's syndrome. Adv Neurol. 2005;96:249-61. Review. PubMed PMID: 16383224.

Cottencin O, Thomas P, Vaiva G, Rascle C, Goudemand M. A case of agitated catatonia. Pharmacopsychiatry. 1999 Jan;32(1):38-40. PubMed PMID: 10071181.

Courtney SM, Petit L, Haxby JV, Ungerleider LG. The role of prefrontal cortex in working memory: examining the contents of consciousness. Philos Trans R Soc Lond B Biol Sci. 1998 Nov 29;353(1377):1819-28. Review. PubMed PMID: 9854254;PubMed Central PMCID: PMC1692423.

Courtney SM, Ungerleider LG. What fMRI has taught us about human vision. Curr Opin Neurobiol. 1997 Aug;7(4):554-61. Review. PubMed PMID: 9287197.

Crawford C, Salmon C. Psychopathology or adaptation? Genetic and evolutionary perspectives on individual differences and psychopathology. Neuro Endocrinol Lett. 2002 Dec;23 Suppl 4:39-45. Review. PubMed PMID: 12496734.

Crespi EJ, Denver RJ. Ancient origins of human developmental plasticity. Am J Hum Biol. 2005 Jan-Feb;17(1):44-54. Review. PubMed PMID: 15611964.

Crinella FM, Beck FW, Robinson JW. Unilateral dominance is not related to neuropsychological integrity. Child Dev. 1971 Dec;42(6):2033-54. Review. PubMed PMID: 5004346.

Crow TJ. March 27, 1827 and what happened later--the impact of psychiatry on evolutionary theory. Prog Neuropsychopharmacol Biol Psychiatry. 2006 Jul;30(5):785-96. Epub 2006 Apr 19. Review. PubMed PMID: 16626847.

Crow TJ. Schizophrenia as the price that homo sapiens pays for language: a resolution of the central paradox in the origin of the species. Brain Res Brain Res Rev. 2000 Mar;31(2-3):118-29. Review. PubMed PMID: 10719140.

Cummings JL, Cunningham K. Obsessive-compulsive disorder in Huntington's disease. Biol Psychiatry. 1992 Feb 1;31(3):263-70. PubMed PMID: 1532132.

Cummings JL, Frankel M. Gilles de la Tourette syndrome and the neurological basis of obsessions and compulsions. Biol Psychiatry. 1985 Oct;20(10):117-26. PubMed PMID: 3862431.

Cuzzillo SL. Historical contingencies in the evolution of human behavior and psychopathology. Psychiatry. 1991 May;54(2):187-207. PubMed PMID: 1852851.

Cybulska EM. The madness of Nietzsche: a misdiagnosis of the millennium? Hosp Med. 2000 Aug;61(8):571-5. PubMed PMID: 11045229.

Cyrulnik B. Ethology of anxiety in phylogeny and ontogeny. Acta Psychiatr Scand Suppl. 1998;393:44-9. PubMed PMID: 9777047.

Cyrulnik B. [Ethology of panic disorders]. Encephale. 1996 Dec;22 SpecNo 5:42-5. Review. French. PubMed PMID: 9138946.

Damasceno A, Delicio AM, Mazo DF, Zullo JF, Scherer P, Ng RT, Damasceno BP. Primitive reflexes and cognitive function. Arq Neuropsiquiatr. 2005 Sep;63(3A):577-82. Epub 2005 Sep 9. PubMed PMID: 16172703.

Darbon P, Scicluna L, Tscherter A, Streit J. Mechanisms controlling bursting activity induced by disinhibition in spinal cord networks. Eur J Neurosci. 2002 Feb;15(4):671-83. PubMed PMID: 11886448.

Dark FL, McGrath JJ, Ron MA. Pathological laughing and crying. Aust N Z J Psychiatry. 1996 Aug;30(4):472-9. Review. PubMed PMID: 8887697.

Darling WG, Hondzinski JM, Harper JG. Gaze direction effects on perceptions of upper limb kinesthetic coordinate system axes. Exp Brain Res. 2000 Dec;135(3):360-72. PubMed PMID: 11146815.

de Andrade ER, Scheuer C. [Analysis of methylphenidate's efficacy using the abbreviated version Conners' questionnaire in attention deficit hyperactivity disorder]. Arq Neuropsiquiatr. 2004 Mar;62(1):81-5. Epub 2004 Apr 28. Portuguese. PubMed PMID: 15122438.

De Grouchy J. Chromosome phylogenies of man, great apes, and Old World monkeys. Genetica. 1987 Aug 31;73(1-2):37-52. Review. PubMed PMID: 3333352.108.

de Jong HA, Sondag EN, Kuipers A, Oosterveld WJ. Swimming behavior of fish. Aviat Space Environ Med. 1996 May;67(5):463-6.

De Lathouwers M, Van Elsacker L. Comparing infant and juvenile behavior in bonobos (Pan paniscus) and chimpanzees (Pan troglodytes): a preliminary study. Primates. 2006 Oct;47(4):287-93. Epub 2006 May 9. PubMed PMID: 16683056.

De Preester H. The deep bodily origins of the subjective perspective: models and their problems. Conscious Cogn. 2007 Sep;16(3):604-18; discussion 619-22. Epub 2007 Jun 21. Review. PubMed PMID: 17590352.

de Waal FB. Darwin's legacy and the study of primate visual communication. Ann N Y Acad Sci. 2003 Dec;1000:7-31. PubMed PMID: 14766618.

Debaere F, Swinnen SP, Béatse E, Sunaert S, Van Hecke P, Duysens J. Brain areas involved in interlimb coordination: a distributed network. Neuroimage. 2001 Nov;14(5):947-58. PubMed PMID: 11697927.

Debray-Ritzen P, Dubois H. [Simple tic disease in children. A report on 93 cases (author's transl)]. Rev Neurol (Paris). 1980;136(1):15-8. French.PubMed PMID: 6771861.

DeLong MR, Alexander GE, Georgopoulos AP, Crutcher MD, Mitchell SJ, Richardson RT. Role of basal ganglia in limb movements. Hum Neurobiol. 1984;2(4):235-44. PubMed PMID: 6715208.

DeLong MR. The neurophysiologic basis of abnormal movements in basal ganglia disorders. Neurobehav Toxicol Teratol. 1983 Nov-Dec;5(6):611-6. Review.

Desgranges B, Eustache F, Rioux P, de La Sayette V, Lechevalier B. Memory disorders in Alzheimer's disease and the organization of human memory. Cortex. 1996 Sep;32(3):387-412. PubMed PMID: 8886519.

Devinsky O, Bear D. Varieties of aggressive behavior in temporal lobe epilepsy. Am J Psychiatry. 1984 May;141(5):651-6. PubMed PMID:6711685.

Dexter DT, Sian J, Rose S, Hindmarsh JG, Mann VM, Cooper JM, Wells FR, Daniel SE, Lees AJ, Schapira AH, et al. Indices of oxidative stress and mitochondrial function in individuals with incidental Lewy body disease. Ann Neurol. 1994 Jan;35(1):38-44. PubMed PMID:8285590.

Dickinson PS. Neuromodulation of central pattern generators in invertebrates and vertebrates. Curr Opin Neurobiol. 2006 Dec;16(6):604-14. Epub 2006 Nov 7. Review. PubMed PMID: 17085040.

Dickinson PS. Interactions among neural networks for behavior. Curr Opin Neurobiol. 1995 Dec;5(6):792-8. Review. PubMed PMID:8805420.121.

Diederich NJ, James Surmeier D, Uchihara T, Grillner S.Goetz CG Parkinson's disease: Is it a consequence of human brain evolution? Mov Disord. 2019 Apr;34(4):453-459. doi: 10.1002/mds.27628. Epub 2019 Feb 13.

Dietrich A. The cognitive neuroscience of creativity. Psychon Bull Rev.2004 Dec;11(6):1011-26. PubMed PMID: 15875970.

Dietrich A. Neurocognitive mechanisms underlying the experience of flow. Conscious Cogn. 2004 Dec;13(4):746-61. Review. PubMed PMID: 15522630.

DiFazio MP, Davis RG. Utility of early single photon emission computed tomography (SPECT) in neonatal gelastic epilepsy associated with hypothalamic hamartoma. J Child Neurol. 2000 Jun;15(6):414-7. PubMed PMID: 10868786.

Dodman, N. H., "Veterinary Models of Obsessive-Compulsive Disorder," Chapter 16, pp. 319-334 In Obsessive-Compulsive Disorders: Practical Management (M. A. Jenike et al., eds.), Moseby, Boston, 1998.

Dopchie N. [Focus on conceptual evolution of the etiology of motor skill disorders]. Brux Med. 1978 Jun;58(6):311-3. French. PubMed PMID: 78750.

Dopson WG, Beckwith BE, Tucker DM, Bullard-Bates PC. Asymmetry of facial expression in spontaneous emotion. Cortex. 1984 Jun;20(2):243-51. PubMedPMID: 6744893.

Durand CM, Kappeler C, Betancur C, Delorme R, Quach H, Goubran-Botros H, Melke J, Nygren G, Chabane N, Bellivier F, Szoke A, Schurhoff F, Rastam M, Anckarsäter H, Gillberg C, Leboyer M, Bourgeron T. Expression and genetic variability of PCDH11Y, a gene specific to Homo sapiens and candidate for susceptibility to psychiatric disorders. Am J Med Genet B Neuropsychiatr Genet. 2006 Jan 5;141B(1):67-70. PubMed PMID: 16331680.

Ebbesson SO. The parcellation theory and its relation to interspecific variability in brain organization, evolutionary and ontogenetic development, and neuronal plasticity. Cell Tissue Res. 1980;213(2):179-212. PubMed PMID: 7459999.

Ecklund-Johnson E, Torres I. Unawareness of deficits in Alzheimer's disease and other dementias: operational definitions and empirical findings. Neuropsychol Rev. 2005 Sep;15(3):147-66. Review. PubMed PMID: 16328733.

Ekman, P., Friesen, W. V., & Ancoli, S. (1980). Facial Signs of Emotional Experience. Journal of Personality and Social Psychology, 39(6), 1125-1134

Ekman P. Darwin, deception, and facial expression. Ann N Y Acad Sci.2003 Dec;1000:205-21. PubMed PMID: 14766633.

Ekstrom SR. The mind beyond our immediate awareness: Freudian, Jungian, and cognitive models of the unconscious. J Anal Psychol. 2004 Nov;49(5):657-82. Review. PubMed PMID: 15533197.

Ellis L. Gender differences in smiling: An evolutionary neuroandrogenic theory. Physiol Behav. 2006 Jul 30;88(4-5):303-8. Epub 2006 Jun 5.Review. PubMedPMID: 16753190.

Eloranta V. Influence of sports background on leg muscle coordination in vertical jumps. Electromyogr Clin Neurophysiol. 2003 Apr-May;43(3):141-56. PubMed PMID: 12712802.

Ettin MF. The spirit of Jungian group psychotherapy: from taboo to totem. Int J Group Psychother. 1995 Oct;45(4):449-70. PubMed PMID: 7558501.

Evidente VG. Is it a tic or Tourette's? Clues for differentiating simplefrom more complex tic disorders. Postgrad Med. 2000 Oct;108(5):175-6, 179-82. Review. PubMed PMID: 11043089.

Faber DP. Jean-Martin Charcot and the epilepsy/hysteria relationship. J Hist Neurosci. 1997 Dec;6(3):275-90. PubMed PMID: 11619864.

Falk D. Prelinguistic evolution in early hominins: whence motherese? Behav Brain Sci. 2004 Aug;27(4):491-503; discussion 503-83. PubMed PMID: 15773427.

Fantini ML, Corona A, Clerici S, Ferini-Strambi L. Aggressive dream content without daytime aggressiveness in REM sleep behavior disorder. Neurology. 2005 Oct 11;65(7):1010-5. PubMed PMID: 16217051.

Favazza AR. The coming of age of self-mutilation. J Nerv Ment Dis. 1998 May;186(5):259-68. Review. PubMed PMID: 9612442.

Fellows SJ, Ernst J, Schwarz M, Töpper R, Noth J. Precision grip deficits in cerebellar disorders in man. Clin Neurophysiol. 2001 Oct;112(10):1793-802. PubMed PMID: 11595136.

Fellows SJ, Noth J, Schwarz M. Precision grip and Parkinson's disease. Brain. 1998 Sep;121 (Pt 9):1771-84. PubMed PMID: 9762964.

Ferrari PF, Coude G, Gallese V, Fogassi L. Having access to others' mind through gaze: the role of ontogenetic and learning processes in gaze-following behavior of macaques. Soc Neurosci. 2008;3(3-4):239-49. PubMed PMID: 18979379.

Finke RA. Imagery, creativity, and emergent structure. Conscious Cogn. 1996 Sep;5(3):381-93. Review. PubMed PMID: 8906409.

Fitch WT. The biology and evolution of music: a comparative perspective. Cognition. 2006 May;100(1):173-215. Epub 2006 Jan 17. Review. PubMedPMID: 16412411.

Flash T, Hochner B. Motor primitives in vertebrates and invertebrates. Curr Opin Neurobiol. 2005 Dec;15(6):660-6. Epub 2005 Nov 4. Review. PubMedPMID: 16275056.

Flashman LA. Disorders of awareness in neuropsychiatric syndromes: an update. Curr Psychiatry Rep. 2002 Oct;4(5):346-53. Review. PubMed PMID: 12230963.

Fletcher AW. Clapping in chimpanzees: evidence of exclusive hand preference in a spontaneous, bimanual gesture. Am J Primatol. 2006 Nov;68(11):1081-8. PubMed PMID: 17044005.

Franssen EH, Kluger A, Torossian CL, Reisberg B. The neurologic syndrome of severe Alzheimer's disease. Relationship to functional decline. Arch Neurol. 1993 Oct;50(10):1029-39. PubMed PMID: 8215960.

Frieling H, Gozner A, Römer KD, Lenz B, Bönsch D, Wilhelm J, Hillemacher T, de Zwaan M, Kornhuber J, Bleich S. Global DNA hypomethylation and DNA hypermethylation of the alpha synuclein promoter in females with anorexia nervosa. Mol Psychiatry. 2007 Mar;12(3):229-30. PubMed PMID: 17325715.

Gallese V, Sinigaglia C. The bodily self as power for action. Neuropsychologia. 2010 Feb;48(3):746-55. Epub 2009 Oct 14. PubMed PMID: 19835895.

Gallese V. Motor abstraction: a neuroscientific account of how action goals and intentions are mapped and understood. Psychol Res. 2009 Jul;73(4):486-98. Epub 2009 Apr 21. Review. PubMed PMID: 19381683.

Gallese V, Rochat M, Cossu G, Sinigaglia C. Motor cognition and its role in the phylogeny and ontogeny of action understanding. Dev Psychol. 2009 Jan;45(1):103-13. Review. PubMed PMID: 19209994.

García Ruiz PJ, Cenjor C, Ulmer E, Hernández J, Cantarero S, Fanjul S, García de Yébenes J. [Speed of ocular saccades in Huntington disease. Prospective study]. Neurologia. 2001 Feb;16(2):70-3. Spanish. PubMed PMID: 11257932.

García-Ribes A, Martí-Carrera I, Martínez-González MJ, Garaizar C, Prats-Viñas JM. [Factors related to the short term remission of tics in children with Tourette syndrome]. Rev Neurol. 2003 Nov 16-30;37(10):901-3. Spanish. PubMed PMID: 14634915.

Gardella E, Rubboli G, Tassinari CA. Ictal grasping: prevalence and characteristics in seizures with different semiology. Epilepsia. 2006;47 Suppl 5:59-63. PubMed PMID: 17239108.

Gardiner K, Costa AC. The proteins of human chromosome 21. Am J Med Genet C Semin Med Genet. 2006 Aug 15;142C(3):196-205. PubMed PMID: 17048356.

Gardner R Jr, Grossman WI, Roffwarg HP, Weiner H. The relationship of small limb movements during REM sleep to dreamed limb action. Psychosom Med. 1975 Mar-Apr;37(2):147-59. PubMed PMID: 166402.

Garfield DA, Gutheil TG. The "whirling dervish" sign in a schizophrenic patient. Hosp Community Psychiatry. 1982 Aug;33(8):658-9. PubMed PMID: 7118103.

Garner JP, Meehan CL, Mench JA. Stereotypies in caged parrots, schizophrenia and autism: evidence for a common mechanism. Behav Brain Res. 2003 Oct 17;145(1-2):125-34. PubMed PMID: 14529811.

Gartner J, Weintraub S, Carlson GA. Childhood-onset psychosis: evolution and comorbidity. Am J Psychiatry. 1997 Feb;154(2):256-61. PubMed PMID: 9016277.

Genovese C. Eros and psychotic despair. Psychoanal Q. 2006 Oct;75(4):1097-129. PubMed PMID: 17094373.

Gervais M, Wilson DS. The evolution and functions of laughter and humor: a synthetic approach. Q Rev Biol. 2005 Dec;80(4):395-430. Review. PubMed PMID:

Ghazanfar AA, Hauser MD. The auditory behaviour of primates: a neuroethological perspective. Curr Opin Neurobiol. 2001 Dec;11(6):712-20. Review. PubMed PMID: 11741023.

Gibson KR. Evolution of human intelligence: the roles of brain size and mental construction. Brain Behav Evol. 2002;59(1-2):10-20. Review. PubMed PMID: 12097857.

Goessler UR, Hein G, Sadick H, Maurer JT, Hörmann K, Verse T. [Physiology, role and neuropharmacology of yawning]. Laryngorhinootologie. 2005 May;84(5):345-51. Review. German. PubMed PMID: 15909246.

Goldenberg G. Imitating gestures and manipulating a mannikin-- the representation of the human body in ideomotor apraxia. Neuropsychologia. 1995 Jan;33(1):63-72. PubMed PMID: 7731541.

Goldin-Meadow S. The development of gesture and speech as an integrated system. New Dir Child Dev. 1998 Spring;(79):29-42. PubMed PMID: 9507702.

Gottlieb GL, Song Q, Hong DA, Corcos DM. Coordinating two degrees of freedom during human arm movement: load and speed invariance of relative joint torques. J Neurophysiol. 1996 Nov;76(5):3196-206. PubMed PMID: 8930266.

Granana N, Tuchman RF. A child with severe head banging. Semin Pediatr Neurol. 1999 Sep;6(3):221-4. PubMed PMID: 10522343.

Green A. [The dead mother]. Psyche (Stuttg). 1993 Mar;47(3):205-40. German. PubMed PMID: 8465007.

Green R. (Serious) sadomasochism: a protected right of privacy? Arch Sex Behav. 2001 Oct;30(5):543-50. PubMed PMID: 11501301.

Grinshpoon A, Barchana M, Ponizovsky A, Lipshitz I, Nahon D, Tal O, Weizman A, Levav I. Cancer in schizophrenia: is the risk higher or lower? Schizophr Res. 2005 Mar 1;73(2-3):333-41. Review. Erratum in: Schizophr Res. 2005 Oct 1;78(1):115-6. PubMed PMID: 15653279.

Gross KB, Skrivanek JA, Carlson KC, Kaufman DM. Familial amyotrophic chorea with acanthocytosis. New clinical and laboratory investigations. Arch Neurol. 1985 Aug;42(8):753-6. PubMed PMID: 4026606.

Grossman WI. Freud's presentation of 'the psychoanalytic mode of thought' in Totem and taboo and his technical papers. Int J Psychoanal. 1998 Jun;79 (Pt 3):469-86. PubMed PMID: 9717096.

Guardiola A, Terra AR, Ferreira LT, Londero RG. [Use of amitriptyline in attention deficit hyperactivity disorder]. Arq Neuropsiquiatr. 1999 Sep;57(3A):599-605. Portuguese. PubMed PMID: 10667283.

Guggisberg AG, Mathis J, Herrmann US, Hess CW. The functional relationship between yawning and vigilance. Behav Brain Res. 2007 Apr 16;179(1):159-66. Epub 2007 Feb 3. PubMed PMID: 17337071.

Guilloteau D, Chalon S. PET and SPECT exploration of central monoaminergic transporters for the development of new drugs and treatments in brain disorders. Curr Pharm Des. 2005;11(25):3237-45. PubMed PMID: 16250852.

Gutiérrez-Alvarez AM. Do your patients suffer from excessive yawning? Acta Psychiatr Scand. 2007 Jan;115(1):80-1. PubMed PMID: 17201870.

Haber SN, Fudge JL. The primate substantia nigra and VTA: integrative circuitry and function. Crit Rev Neurobiol. 1997;11(4):323-42. Review. PubMed PMID: 9336716.

Haber SN, Fudge JL. The interface between dopamine neurons and the amygdala: implications for schizophrenia. Schizophr Bull. 1997;23(3):471-82. Review. PubMed PMID: 9327510.

Hanly MA. Sado-masochism in Charlotte Brontë's Jane Eyre: a ridge of lighted health. Int J Psychoanal. 1993 Oct;74 (Pt 5):1049-61. PubMed PMID: 8307694.

Harris-Warrick RM, Marder E. Modulation of neural networks for behavior. Annu Rev Neurosci. 1991;14:39-57. Review. PubMed PMID: 2031576.

Hashimoto R, Yoshida M, Tanaka Y. Utilization behavior after right thalamic infarction. Eur Neurol. 1995;35(1):58-62. PubMed PMID: 7737250.

Hausdorff JM, Yogev G, Springer S, Simon ES, Giladi N. Walking is more like catching than tapping: gait in the elderly as a complex cognitive task. Exp Brain Res. 2005 Aug;164(4):541-8. Epub 2005 Apr 28. PubMed PMID: 15864565.

Hauser MD. Right hemisphere dominance for the production of facial expression in monkeys. Science. 1993 Jul 23;261(5120):475-7. PubMed PMID:

Hecht GM. ADHD as a disorder of adaptation. J Am Acad Child Adolesc Psychiatry. 1998 Aug;37(8):799; author reply 799-800. PubMed PMID: 9695439.

Heesy CP, Ross CF. Evolution of activity patterns and chromatic vision in primates: morphometrics, genetics and cladistics. J Hum Evol. 2001 Feb;40(2):111-49. Erratum in: J Hum Evol 2001 Sep;41(3):253. PubMed PMID: 11161957.

Heim R. [Patricide and the dialectics of enlightenment. The "fatherless society" as a model of psychoanalytic archaeology of modern times]. Psyche (Stuttg). 1993 Apr;47(4):344-77. German. PubMed PMID: 8502759.

Helvink B, Holroyd S. Buspirone for stereotypic movements in elderly with cognitive impairment. J Neuropsychiatry Clin Neurosci. 2006 Spring;18(2):242-4. PubMed PMID: 16720804.

Hermann I. Clinging-going-in-search. A contrasting pair of instincts and their relation to sadism and masochism. Psychoanal Q. 1976 Jan;45(1):5-36. PubMed PMID: 942796.

Hermelin B, O'Connor N, Lee S, Treffert D. Intelligence and musical improvisation. Psychol Med. 1989 May;19(2):447-57. PubMed PMID: 2762446.

Herrero MT, Barcia C, Navarro JM. Functional anatomy of thalamus and basal ganglia. Childs Nerv Syst. 2002 Aug;18(8):386-404. Epub 2002 Jul 26. Review. PubMed PMID: 12192499.

Hirsch EC, Graybiel AM, Duyckaerts C, Javoy-Agid F. Neuronal loss in the pedunculopontine tegmental nucleus in Parkinson disease and in progressive supranuclear palsy. Proc Natl Acad Sci U S A. 1987 Aug;84(16):5976-80. PubMed PMID: 3475716; PubMed Central PMCID: PMC298986.

Hobson JA, McCarley RW. The brain as a dream state generator: an activation-synthesis hypothesis of the dream process. Am J Psychiatry. 1977 Dec;134(12):1335-48. PubMed PMID: 21570.

Hofer MA. Unexplained infant crying: an evolutionary perspective. Acta Paediatr. 2002;91(5):491-6. Review. PubMed PMID: 12113311.

Hogenson GB. Archetypes as action patterns. J Anal Psychol.2009 Jun;54(3):325-37. PubMed PMID: 19531123.

Holguín JA. [Autism of unknown aetiology]. Rev Neurol. 2003 Aug 1-15;37(3):259-66. Review. Spanish. PubMed PMID: 12938058.

Holmes KR. Freud, evolution, and the tragedy of man. J Am Psychoanal Assoc. 1983;31(1):187-210. PubMed PMID: 6681416.

Holmquist R, Miyamoto MM, Goodman M. Higher-primate phylogeny—why can't we decide? Mol Biol Evol. 1988 May;5(3):201-16. PubMed PMID:3133535.

Hopkins WD. Comparative and familial analysis of handedness in great apes. Psychol Bull. 2006 Jul;132(4):538-59. PubMed PMID: 16822166; PubMed Central PMCID: PMC2063575.

Hopkins WD, Russell JL, Cantalupo C, Freeman H, Schapiro SJ. Factors influencing the prevalence and handedness for throwing in captive chimpanzees (Pan troglodytes). J Comp Psychol. 2005 Nov;119(4):363-70. PubMed PMID: 16366769; PubMed Central PMCID: PMC2680150.

Hopkins WD, Russell JL. Further evidence of a right hand advantage in motor skill by chimpanzees (Pan troglodytes). Neuropsychologia. 2004;42(7):990-6. PubMed PMID: 14998713.

Hore J, Watts S, Tweed D, Miller B. Overarm throws with the nondominant arm: kinematics of accuracy. J Neurophysiol. 1996 Dec;76(6):3693-704. PubMed PMID: 8985867.

Hore J. Motor control, excitement, and overarm throwing. Can J Physiol Pharmacol. 1996 Apr;74(4):385-9. Review. PubMed PMID:8828885.

Hoshi E, Tanji J. Differential roles of neuronal activity in thesupplementary and presupplementary motor areas: from information retrieval to motor planning and execution. J Neurophysiol. 2004 Dec;92(6):3482-99. Epub 2004 Jul 21. PubMed PMID: 15269227.

Iacoboni M, Mazziotta JC. Mirror neuron system: basic findings and clinical applications. Ann Neurol. 2007 Sep;62(3):213-8. Review. PubMed PMID:17721988.

Ilinsky IA, Tourtellotte WG, Kultas-Ilinsky K. Anatomical distinctions between the two basal ganglia afferent territories in the primate motor thalamus. Stereotact Funct Neurosurg. 1993;60(1-3):62-9. PubMed PMID:8511434.

Isaacs KL, Barr WB, Nelson PK, Devinsky O. Degree of handedness andcerebral dominance. Neurology. 2006 Jun 27;66(12):1855-8. PubMed PMID: 16801650.

Isoda M, Tanji J. Cellular activity in the supplementary eye field during sequential performance of multiple saccades. J Neurophysiol. 2002 Dec;88(6):3541-5. PubMed PMID: 12466467.

Iverson JM, Longobardi E, Caselli MC. Relationship between gestures and words in children with Down's syndrome and typically developing children in the early stages of communicative development. Int J Lang Commun Disord. 2003 Apr-Jun;38(2):179-97. PubMed PMID: 12745936.

Iwase M, Ouchi Y, Okada H, Yokoyama C, Nobezawa S, Yoshikawa E, Tsukada H,Takeda M, Yamashita K, Takeda M, Yamaguti K, Kuratsune H, Shimizu A, Watanabe Y. Neural substrates of human facial expression of pleasant emotion induced by comic films: a PET Study. Neuroimage. 2002 Oct;17(2):758-68.PubMed PMID: 12377151.

Jaeger D, Gilman S, Aldridge JW. Primate basal ganglia activity in a precued reaching task: preparation for movement. Exp Brain Res. 1993;95(1):51-64.PubMed PMID: 8405253.

Jahanshahi M, Jenkins IH, Brown RG, Marsden CD, Passingham RE, Brooks DJ. Self-initiated versus externally triggered movements. I. An investigation using measurement of regional cerebral blood flow with PET and movement-related potentials in normal and Parkinson's disease subjects. Brain. 1995 Aug;118 (Pt 4):913-33. PubMed PMID: 7655888.

Janković SM, Sokić DV, Vojvodić NM, Ristić AJ. [The first film presentation of REM sleep behavior disorder precedes its scientific debut by 35 years]. Srp Arh Celok Lek. 2006 Sep-Oct;134(9-10):466-9. Serbian. PubMed PMID:17252919.

Jensen PS, Mrazek D, Knapp PK, Steinberg L, Pfeffer C, Schowalter J, ShapiroT. Evolution and revolution in child psychiatry: ADHD as a disorder of adaptation. J Am Acad Child Adolesc Psychiatry. 1997 Dec;36(12):1672-9; discussion 1679-81. Review. PubMed PMID: 9401328.

Joel D, Weiner I. The connections of the primate subthalamic nucleus: indirect pathways and the open-interconnected scheme of basal ganglia-thalamocortical circuitry. Brain Res Brain Res Rev. 1997 Feb;23(1-2):62-78. Review. PubMed PMID: 9063587.

Joffe TH, Dunbar RI. Visual and socio-cognitive information processing in primate brain evolution. Proc Biol Sci. 1997 Sep 22;264(1386):1303-7. PubMed PMID: 9332015; PubMed Central PMCID: PMC1688580.

Johnson J. Catatonia: the tension insanity. Br J Psychiatry. 1993 Jun;162:733-8. Review. PubMed PMID: 8330104.

Jones S, Martin R, Pilbeam D Human Evolution Cambridge UniversityPress Cambridge, UK 1992

Joseph R. Frontal lobe psychopathology: mania, depression, confabulation, catatonia, perseveration, obsessive compulsions, and schizophrenia. Psychiatry. 1999 Summer;62(2):138-72. Review. PubMed PMID: 10420428.

Josephs KA, Whitwell JL, Boeve BF, Knopman DS, Tang-Wai DF, Drubach DA, JackCR Jr, Petersen RC. Visual hallucinations in posterior cortical atrophy. Arch Neurol. 2006 Oct;63(10):1427-32. PubMed PMID: 17030659; PubMed Central PMCID: PMC2748870.

Joyce JN. Multiple dopamine receptors and behavior. Neurosci Biobehav Rev. 1983 Summer;7(2):227-56. Review. PubMed PMID:6136014.

Juda DP. Exorcising Freud's "daemonic" compulsion to repeat: repetition compulsion as part of the adaptational/maturational process. J Am Acad Psychoanal. 1983 Jul;11(3):353-75. PubMed PMID:6874460.

Jueptner M, Weiller C. A review of differences between basal ganglia and cerebellar control of movements as revealed by functional imaging studies. Brain. 1998 Aug;121 (Pt 8):1437-49. Review. PubMed PMID:9712006.

Jueptner M, Frith CD, Brooks DJ, Frackowiak RS, Passingham RE. Anatomy of motor learning. II. Subcortical structures and learning by trial and error. J Neurophysiol. 1997 Mar;77(3):1325-37. PubMed PMID:9084600.

Jürgens U, Müller-Preuss P. Convergent projections of different limbic vocalization areas in the squirrel monkey. Exp Brain Res. 1977 Aug 8;29(1):75-83. PubMed PMID: 408164.

Kaas JH, Hackett TA. Subdivisions of auditory cortex and processing streams in primates. Proc Natl Acad Sci U S A. 2000 Oct 24;97(22):11793-9. PubMed PMID: 11050211; PubMed Central PMCID:PMC34351.

Kalaska JF, Scott SH, Cisek P, Sergio LE. Cortical control of reaching movements. Curr Opin Neurobiol. 1997 Dec;7(6):849-59. Review. PubMedPMID: 9464979.

Kalin NH, Shelton SE. Ontogeny and stability of separation andthreat-induced defensive behaviors in rhesus monkeys during the first year of life. Am J Primatol. 1998;44(2):125-35. PubMed PMID:9503124.

Kalin NH, Shelton SE, Snowdon CT. Affiliative vocalizations in infant rhesus macaques (Macaca mulatta). J Comp Psychol. 1992 Sep;106(3):254-61. PubMed PMID:1395495.

Katz PS. Neurons, networks, and motor behavior. Neuron. 1996 Feb;16(2):245-53. Review. PubMed PMID:8789940.

Kernberg OF. Sadomasochism, sexual excitement, and perversion. J Am Psychoanal Assoc. 1991;39(2):333-62. PubMed PMID: 1856437.

Kertesz A, McMonagle P, Blair M, Davidson W, Munoz DG. The evolution and pathology of frontotemporal dementia. Brain. 2005 Sep;128(Pt 9):1996-2005. Epub 2005 Jul 20. PubMed PMID: 16033782.

Keverne EB, Martel FL, Nevison CM. Primate brain evolution: genetic and functional considerations. Proc Biol Sci. 1996 Jun 22;263(1371):689-96. PubMed PMID: 8763791.

Kievit J, Kuypers HG. Basal forebrain and hypothalamic connection to frontal and parietal cortex in the Rhesus monkey. Science. 1975 Feb 21;187(4177):660-2. PubMed PMID: 1114317.

Kingsbury MA, Yung YC, Peterson SE, Westra JW, Chun J. Aneuploidy in the normal and diseased brain. Cell Mol Life Sci. 2006 Nov;63(22):2626-41. Review. PubMed PMID: 16952055.

Kirk EC, Cartmill M, Kay RF, Lemelin P. Comment on "Grasping primate origins". Science. 2003 May 2;300(5620):741; author reply 741. PubMed PMID: 12730582.

Kjaerulff O, Kiehn O. Crossed rhythmic synaptic input to motoneurons during selective activation of the contralateral spinal locomotor network. J Neurosci. 1997 Dec 15;17(24):9433-47. PubMed PMID: 9390999.

Klar AJ. Genetic models for handedness, brain lateralization, schizophrenia, and manic-depression. Schizophr Res. 1999 Oct 19;39(3):207-18. Review. PubMed PMID: 10507513.

Knox J. Mirror neurons and embodied simulation in the development of archetypes and self-agency. J Anal Psychol. 2009 Jun;54(3):307-23. PubMed PMID: 19531122.

Kollár K, Jelenik Z, Hegelsberger E. [Neurologic aspects of HIV infections--follow-up of pediatric patients]. Ideggyogy Sz. 2003 Nov 20;56(11-12):397-404. Hungarian. Erratum in: Ideggyogy Sz. 2004 Jan 20;57(1-2):54. PubMed PMID: 14743594.

Konarski JZ, McIntyre RS, Grupp LA, Kennedy SH. Is the cerebellum relevant in the circuitry of neuropsychiatric disorders? J Psychiatry Neurosci. 2005 May;30(3):178-86. Review. PubMed PMID: 15944742; PubMed Central PMCID: PMC1089778.

Konczak J, Borutta M, Dichgans J. The development of goal-directed reaching in infants. II. Learning to produce task-adequate patterns of joint torque. Exp Brain Res. 1997 Mar;113(3):465-74. PubMed PMID: 9108213.

Koop BF, Tagle DA, Goodman M, Slightom JL. A molecular view of primate phylogeny and important systematic and evolutionary questions. Mol Biol Evol. 1989 Nov;6(6):580-612. PubMed PMID: 2488474.

Kristiansen LV, Meador-Woodruff JH. Abnormal striatal expression of transcripts encoding NMDA interacting PSD proteins in schizophrenia, bipolar disorder and major depression. Schizophr Res. 2005 Oct 1;78(1):87-93. PubMed PMID: 16023328.

Kudriavtseva NN, Bakshtanovskaia IV. [The neurochemical control of aggression and submission]. Zh Vyssh Nerv Deiat Im I P Pavlova. 1991 May-Jun;41(3):459-66. Russian. PubMed PMID: 1681631.

Kudriavtseva NN, Bakshtanovskaia IV, Popova NK. [Catatonia as an element of submissive behavior in mice during interspecies agonistic interactions]. Zh Vyssh Nerv Deiat Im I P Pavlova. 1989 Jan-Feb;39(1):128-36. Russian. PubMed PMID: 2735117.

Kuypers FA, Yuan J, Lewis RA, Snyder LM, Kiefer CR, Bunyaratvej A, Fucharoen S, Ma L, Styles L, de Jong K, Schrier SL. Membrane phospholipid asymmetry in human thalassemia. Blood. 1998 Apr 15;91(8):3044-51. PubMed PMID: 9531618.

Lakoff A. Adaptive will: the evolution of attention deficit disorder. J Hist Behav Sci. 2000 Spring;36(2):149-69. PubMed PMID: 10797349.

Laplane D, Levasseur M, Pillon B, Dubois B, Baulac M, Mazoyer B, Tran DinhS, Sette G, Danze F, Baron JC. Obsessive-compulsive and other behavioural changes with bilateral basal ganglia lesions. A neuropsychological, magnetic resonance imaging and positron tomography study. Brain. 1989 Jun;112 (Pt 3):699-725. PubMed PMID: 2786440.

Lasker AG, Zee DS, Hain TC, Folstein SE, Singer HS. Saccades in Huntington's disease: slowing and dysmetria. Neurology. 1988 Mar;38(3):427-31. PubMed PMID: 2964566.

Lavrysen A, Elliott D, Buekers MJ, Feys P, Helsen WF. Eye-hand coordination asymmetries in manual aiming. J Mot Behav. 2007 Jan;39(1):9-18. PubMed PMID: 17251167.

Leckman JF, Bloch MH, Scahill L, King RA. Tourette syndrome: the self under siege. J Child Neurol. 2006 Aug;21(8):642-9. Review. PubMed PMID: 16970864.

Leckman JF. Phenomenology of tics and natural history of tic disorders. Brain Dev. 2003 Dec;25 Suppl 1:S24-8. Review. PubMed PMID: 14980368.

LeCroy D. Freud: the first evolutionary psychologist? Ann N Y Acad Sci. 2000 Apr;907:182-90. PubMed PMID: 10818628.

Legrand D. Pre-reflective self-as-subject from experiential and empirical perspectives. Conscious Cogn. 2007 Sep;16(3):583-99. Epub 2007 May 29. Review. PubMed PMID: 17533140.

Leichnetz GR, Goldberg ME. Higher centers concerned with eye movement and visual attention: cerebral cortex and thalamus. Rev Oculomot Res. 1988;2:365-429. Review. PubMed PMID: 3153653.

Leonards U, Scott-Samuel NE. Idiosyncratic initiation of saccadic face exploration in humans. Vision Res. 2005 Sep;45(20):2677-84. Epub 2005 Apr 18. PubMed PMID: 16042969.

Leung SK, Ungvari GS, Ng FS, Cheung HK, Leung T. Tardive dyskinesia in Chinese inpatients with chronic schizophrenia. Prog Neuropsychopharmacol Biol Psychiatry. 2003 Sep;27(6):1029-35. PubMed PMID: 14499321.

Levy MS. A conceptualization of the repetition compulsion. Psychiatry. 2000 Spring;63(1):45-53. Review. PubMed PMID: 10855759.

Libbrecht K, Quackelbeen J. On the early history of male hysteria and psychic trauma. Charcot's influence on Freudian thought. J Hist Behav Sci. 1995 Oct;31(4):370-84. PubMed PMID: 8551015.

Lichter DG, Jackson LA, Schachter M. Clinical evidence of genomic imprinting in Tourette's syndrome. Neurology. 1995 May;45(5):924-8. PubMed PMID: 7746408.

Lieberman P. On the nature and evolution of the neural bases of human language. Am J Phys Anthropol. 2002;Suppl 35:36-62. Review. PubMed PMID: 12653308.

Lochner C, Hemmings SM, Kinnear CJ, Niehaus DJ, Nel DG, Corfield VA, Moolman-Smook JC, Seedat S, Stein DJ. Cluster analysis of obsessive-compulsive spectrum disorders in patients with obsessive-compulsive disorder: clinical and genetic correlates. Compr Psychiatry. 2005 Jan-Feb;46(1):14-9. PubMed PMID: 15714189.

Lopez OL, Wisniewski SR, Becker JT, Boller F, DeKosky ST. Psychiatric medication and abnormal behavior as predictors of progression in probable Alzheimer disease. Arch Neurol. 1999 Oct;56(10):1266-72. PubMed PMID: 10520944.

Lopez OL, Wisnieski SR, Becker JT, Boller F, DeKosky ST. Extrapyramidal signs in patients with probable Alzheimer disease. Arch Neurol. 1997 Aug;54(8):969-75. PubMed PMID: 9267971.

Lyons DE, Santos LR, Keil FC. Reflections of other minds: how primate social cognition can inform the function of mirror neurons. Curr Opin Neurobiol. 2006 Apr;16(2):230-4. Epub 2006 Mar 27. Review. PubMed PMID: 16564687; PubMed Central PMCID: PMC1764824.

Machado CJ, Bachevalier J. Non-human primate models of childhood psychopathology: the promise and the limitations. J Child Psychol Psychiatry. 2003 Jan;44(1):64-87. Review. PubMed PMID: 12553413.

Maestripieri D. Primate cognition and the bared-teeth display: a reevaluation of the concept of formal dominance. J Comp Psychol. 1996 Dec;110(4):402-5. Review. PubMed PMID: 8956510.

Mai R, Sartori I, Francione S, Tassi L, Castana L, Cardinale F, Cossu M, Citterio A, Colombo N, Lo Russo G, Nobili L. Sleep-related hyperkinetic seizures: always a frontal onset? Neurol Sci. 2005 Dec;26 Suppl 3:s220-4. PubMed PMID: 16331400.

Mair WG, Warrington EK, Weiskrantz L. Memory disorder in Korsakoff's psychosis: a neuropathological and neuropsychological investigation of two cases. Brain. 1979 Dec;102(4):749-83. PubMed PMID: 116710.

Makari GJ. German philosophy, Freud, and the riddle of the woman. J Am Psychoanal Assoc. 1991;39(1):183-213. Review. PubMed PMID: 2026851.

Malinowski B Coral gardens and their magic. 1966 Allen and Unwin.

Manchanda SK, Poddar A, Saha S, Bhatia SC, Kumar VM, Nayar U. Predatory aggression induced by hypothalamic stimulation: modulation by midbrain periaqueductal gray (PAG). Neurobiology (Bp). 1995;3(3-4):405-17. PubMed PMID: 8696308.

Marantz AG, Verghese J. Capgras' syndrome in dementia with Lewy bodies. J Geriatr Psychiatry Neurol. 2002 Winter;15(4):239-41. PubMed PMID: 12489921.

Marder E, Bucher D. Central pattern generators and the control of rhythmic movements. Curr Biol. 2001 Nov 27;11(23):R986-96. Review. PubMed PMID: 11728329.

Markiewicz MR, Ohrbach R, McCall WD Jr. Oral behaviors checklist: reliability of performance in targeted waking-state behaviors. J Orofac Pain. 2006 Fall;20(4):306-16. PubMed PMID: 17190029.

Marsden CD, Obeso JA. The functions of the basal ganglia and the paradox of stereotaxic surgery in Parkinson's disease. Brain. 1994 Aug;117 (Pt 4):877-97.Review. PubMed PMID: 7922472.

Martel FL, Nevison CM, Rayment FD, Simpson MJ, Keverne EB. Opioid receptor blockade reduces maternal affect and social grooming in rhesus monkeys. Psychoneuroendocrinology. 1993;18(4):307-21. PubMed PMID: 8391149.

Martinez J, Dugaiczyk LJ, Zielinski R, Dugaiczyk A. Human genetic disorders, a phylogenetic perspective. J Mol Biol. 2001 May 11;308(4):587-96. PubMed PMID: 11350162.

Matejcek Z. Is ADHD adaptive or non-adaptive behavior? Neuro Endocrinol Lett. 2003 Jun-Aug;24(3-4):148-50. PubMed PMID: 14523348

Matson JL, Hamilton M, Duncan D, Bamburg J, Smiroldo B, Anderson S, BaglioC. Characteristics of stereotypic movement disorder and self-injurious behavior assessed with the Diagnostic Assessment for the Severely Handicapped (DASH-II). Res Dev Disabil. 1997 Nov-Dec;18(6):457-69. PubMed PMID: 9403928.

Matsumoto D, Willingham B. The thrill of victory and the agony of defeat: spontaneous expressions of medal winners of the 2004 Athens Olympic Games. J PersSoc Psychol. 2006 Sep;91(3):568-81. PubMed PMID: 16938038.

Mauguiere F. [Control of visual exploration: anatomic and physiologic data]. J Fr Ophtalmol. 1985;8(12):803-12. French. PubMed PMID: 3938788.

Maurizi CP. Influenza and schizophrenia: a possible connection with the substantia nigra. Med Hypotheses. 1984 Oct;15(2):163-7. PubMed PMID: 6096682.

McGaugh JL, Cahill L, Roozendaal B. Involvement of the amygdala in memory storage: interaction with other brain systems. Proc Natl Acad Sci U S A. 1996 Nov 26;93(24):13508-14. Review. PubMed PMID: 8942964; PubMed Central PMCID: PMC33638.

McGrath CM, Kennedy RE, Hoye W, Yablon SA. Stereotypic movementdisorder after acquired brain injury. Brain Inj. 2002 May;16(5):447-51. PubMed PMID: 12097226.

McManus IC, Drury H. The handedness of Leonardo da Vinci: a tale of the complexities of lateralisation. Brain Cogn. 2004 Jul;55(2):262-8. PubMedPMID: 15177791.

McMullen T. The savant syndrome and extrasensory perception. Psychol Rep. 1991 Dec;69(3 Pt 1):1004-6. PubMed PMID: 1784646.

Mead M Totem and Taboo reconsidered with respect. Bull Menninger Clin. 1963 Jul;27:185-99. PubMed PMID: 13934295.

Meeks TW, Ropacki SA, Jeste DV. The neurobiology of neuropsychiatric syndromes in dementia. Curr Opin Psychiatry. 2006 Nov;19(6):581-6. Review. PubMedPMID: 17012935.

Mellerup E, Kristesen F. Mania as a dysfunction of reentry: application of Edelman's and Tononi's hypothesis for consciousness in relation to a psychiatric disorder. Med Hypotheses. 2004;63(3):464-6. PubMed PMID: 15288370.

Mendez MF, Mirea A. Adult head-banging and stereotypic movement disorders. Mov Disord. 1998 Sep;13(5):825-8. PubMed PMID: 9756153.

Miguel EC, do Rosário-Campos MC, Prado HS, do Valle R, Rauch SL, Coffey BJ, Baer L, Savage CR, O'Sullivan RL, Jenike MA, Leckman JF. Sensory phenomena in obsessive-compulsive disorder and Tourette's disorder. J Clin Psychiatry. 2000 Feb;61(2):150-6; quiz 157. PubMed PMID: 10732667.

Miklósi A, Soproni K. A comparative analysis of animals' understanding of the human pointing gesture. Anim Cogn. 2006 Apr;9(2):81-93. Epub 2005 Oct 19. Review. PubMed PMID: 16235075.

Miller A. Pseudobulbar affect in multiple sclerosis: toward the development of innovative therapeutic strategies. J Neurol Sci. 2006 Jun 15;245(1-2):153-9. Epub 2006 May 3. Review. PubMed PMID: 16674978.

Miller SA, Jones MD. Kinematics of four methods of stabbing: a preliminary study. Forensic Sci Int. 1996 Sep 30;82(2):183-90. PubMed PMID: 8885377.

Mitterauer B. An interdisciplinary approach towards a theory of consciousness. Biosystems. 1998 Feb;45(2):99-121. PubMed PMID: 9544402.

Modell JG, Mountz JM, Curtis GC, Greden JF. Neurophysiologic dysfunction in basal ganglia/limbic striatal and thalamocortical circuits as a pathogenetic mechanism of obsessive-compulsive disorder. J Neuropsychiatry Clin Neurosci. 1989 Winter;1(1):27-36. Review. PubMed PMID: 2535426.

Montagu A Touching Harper and Row Third Edition New York 1986.

Moran, M "Autistic Savant Made Famous by 'Rain Man' Dies-What is New in Understanding of Syndrome" in Neurology Today 2010 Feb 10(3): 14-15

Morrison PR. Distance cues and depth avoidance on the visual cliff. Percept Mot Skills. 1982 Jun;54(3 Pt 2):1195-8. PubMed PMID: 7110861.

Moskowitz AK. "Scared stiff": catatonia as an evolutionary-based fear response. Psychol Rev. 2004 Oct;111(4):984-1002. Review. PubMedPMID: 15482070.

Mozaz M, Garaigordobil M, Gonzalez Rothi LJ, Anderson J, Crucian GP, Heilman KM. Posture recognition in Alzheimer's disease. Brain Cogn. 2006 Dec;62(3):241-5. Epub 2006 Oct 5. PubMed PMID: 17027133.

Mozaz M, Rothi LJ, Anderson JM, Crucian GP, Heilman KM. Postural knowledge of transitive pantomimes and intransitive gestures. J Int Neuropsychol Soc. 2002 Nov;8(7):958-62. PubMed PMID: 12405548.

Munhoz RP, Lang AE. Gestes antagonistes in psychogenic dystonia. Mov Disord. 2004 Mar;19(3):331-2. PubMed PMID: 15022189.

Muscarella F, Fink B, Grammer K, Kirk-Smith M. Homosexual orientation in males: evolutionary and ethological aspects. Neuro Endocrinol Lett. 2001 Dec;22(6):393-400. Review. PubMed PMID: 11781535.

Mustanski BS, Chivers ML, Bailey JM. A critical review of recent biological research on human sexual orientation. Annu Rev Sex Res. 2002;13:89-140. Review. PubMed PMID: 12836730.

Nahon JL. Birth of 'human-specific' genes during primate evolution. Genetica. 2003 Jul;118(2-3):193-208. Review. PubMed PMID: 12868609.

Nakayama K, Nishimaru H, Kudo N. Developmental changes in 5-hydroxytryptamine-induced rhythmic activity in the spinal cord of rat fetuses in vitro. Neurosci Lett. 2001 Jul 6;307(1):1-4. PubMed PMID: 11516560.

Nicholls ME, Ellis BE, Clement JG, Yoshino M. Detecting hemifacial asymmetries in emotional expression with three-dimensional computerized image analysis. Proc Biol Sci. 2004 Apr 7;271(1540):663-8. PubMed PMID: 15209097; PubMed Central PMCID: PMC1691649.

Nieoullon A. Dopamine and the regulation of cognition and attention. Prog Neurobiol. 2002 May;67(1):53-83. Review. PubMed PMID: 12126656.

Nishikawa KC. Evolutionary convergence in nervous systems: insights from comparative phylogenetic studies. Brain Behav Evol. 2002;59(5-6):240-9. PubMed PMID: 12207081.

O'Neill M, Bard KA, Linnell M, Fluck M. Maternal gestures with 20-month-old infants in two contexts. Dev Sci. 2005 Jul;8(4):352-9. PubMed PMID: 15985069.

Ohara K, Morita Y. [Case with probable dementia with Lewy bodies, who shows reduplicative paramnesia and Capgras syndrome]. Seishin Shinkeigaku Zasshi. 2006;108(7):705-14. Japanese. PubMed PMID: 16999337.

Orlandini A. Repetition compulsion in a trauma victim: is the "analgesia principle" beyond the pleasure principle? Clinical implications. J Am Acad Psychoanal Dyn Psychiatry. 2004 Fall;32(3):525-40. Review. PubMed PMID: 15451684.

Orth M, Trimble MR. Friedrich Nietzsche's mental illness--general paralysis of the insane vs. frontotemporal dementia. Acta Psychiatr Scand. 2006 Dec;114(6):439-44; discussion 445. PubMed PMID: 17087793.

Otapowicz D, Sobaniec W, Kułak W, Okurowska-Zawada B. Time of cooing appearance and further development of speech in children with cerebral palsy. Rocz Akad Med Bialymst. 2005;50 Suppl 1:78-81. PubMed PMID: 16119633.

Owen AM, Coleman MR, Boly M, Davis MH, Laureys S, Pickard JD. Detecting awareness in the vegetative state. Science. 2006 Sep 8;313(5792):1402.PubMed PMID: 16959998.

Ozçalişkan S, Goldin-Meadow S. Gesture is at the cutting edge of early language development. Cognition. 2005 Jul;96(3):B101-13. Epub 2005 Mar 23. PubMedPMID: 15996556.

Panksepp J, Burgdorf J. "Laughing" rats and the evolutionary antecedentsofhuman joy? Physiol Behav. 2003 Aug;79(3):533-47. Review. PubMed PMID: 12954448.

Papanikolaou EG, Platteau P, Albano C, Kolibianakis E, Devroey P. Achievement of pregnancy three times in the same patient during luteal GnRH agonist administration. Reprod Biomed Online. 2005 Mar;10(3):347-9. PubMed PMID: 15820040.

Parent A. The brain in evolution and involution. Biochem CellBiol. 1997;75(6):651-67. Review. PubMed PMID: 9599655.

Pates J, Maynard I. Effects of hypnosis on flow states and golf performance. Percept Mot Skills. 2000 Dec;91(3 Pt 2):1057-75. PubMed PMID:11219648.

Pearce JM. Some neurological aspects of laughter. Eur Neurol. 2004;52(3):169-71. Epub 2004 Nov 2. Review. PubMed PMID:15528918.

Pearson K. Motor systems. Curr Opin Neurobiol. 2000 Oct;10(5):649-54. Review. PubMed PMID: 11084328.

Pearson KG. Neural adaptation in the generation of rhythmic behavior. Annu Rev Physiol. 2000;62:723-53. Review. PubMed PMID:10845109.

Pearson KG. Common principles of motor control in vertebrates and invertebrates. Annu Rev Neurosci. 1993;16:265-97. Review. PubMedPMID: 8460894.

Persad SM, Polivy J. Differences between depressed and nondepressed individuals in the recognition of and response to facial emotional cues. J Abnorm Psychol. 1993 Aug;102(3):358-68. PubMed PMID:8408947.

Pettersson AF, Olsson E, Wahlund LO. Motor function in subjects with mild cognitive impairment and early Alzheimer's disease. Dement Geriatr CognDisord. 2005;19(5-6):299-304. Epub 2005 Mar 22. PubMed PMID:15785030.

Peña F, García O. Breathing generation and potential pharmacotherapeutic approaches to central respiratory disorders. Curr Med Chem. 2006;13(22):2681-93. Review. PubMed PMID: 17017919.

Pigeon P, Bortolami SB, DiZio P, Lackner JR. Coordinated turn-and-reach movements. I. Anticipatory compensation for self-generated coriolis and interaction torques. J Neurophysiol. 2003 Jan;89(1):276-89. PubMed PMID: 12522179.

Pineda JA, Hecht E. Mirroring and mu rhythm involvement in social cognition: are there dissociable subcomponents of theory of mind? Biol Psychol. 2009 Mar;80(3):306-14. Epub 2008 Nov 21. PubMed PMID:19063933.

Ploog D. Neurobiology of primate audio-vocal behavior. Brain Res. 1981 Aug;228(1):35-61. Review. PubMed PMID:7023614.

Ploog D. Phonation, emotion, cognition, with reference to the brain mechanisms involved. Ciba Found Symp. 1979;(69):79-98. PubMed PMID: 121283.

Pomerleau CS. Co-factors for smoking and evolutionary psychobiology. Addiction. 1997 Apr;92(4):397-408. Review. PubMed PMID: 9177061.

Pompeiano O. The control of posture and movements during REM sleep: neurophysiological and neurochemical mechanisms. Acta Astronaut. 1975 Mar-Apr;2(3-4):225-39. PubMed PMID: 11887914.

Pontius AA. Neuroethics vs neurophysiologically and neuropsychologically uninformed influences in child-rearing, education, emerging hunter-gatherers, and artificial intelligence models of the brain. Psychol Rep. 1993 Apr;72(2):451-8. PubMed PMID: 8488227.

Poulin-Dubois D, Brooker I, Chow V. The developmental origins of naïve psychology in infancy. Adv Child Dev Behav. 2009;37:55-104. Review. PubMed PMID: 19673160.

Povinelli DJ, Eddy TJ. What young chimpanzees know about seeing. Monogr Soc Res Child Dev. 1996;61(3):i-vi, 1-152; discussion 153-91. PubMed PMID: 8795292.

Pozzo T, Levik Y, Berthoz A. Head and trunk movements in the frontal plane during complex dynamic equilibrium tasks in humans. Exp Brain Res. 1995;106(2):327-38. PubMed PMID: 8566197.

Preuschoft H. Mechanisms for the acquisition of habitual bipedality:are there biomechanical reasons for the acquisition of upright bipedal posture? J Anat. 2004 May;204(5):363-84. Review. PubMed PMID: 15198701; PubMedCentral PMCID: PMC1571303.

Rader N, Bausano M, Richards JE. On the nature of the visual-cliff-avoidance response in human infants. Child Dev. 1980 Mar;51(1):61-8. PubMed PMID: 7363749.

Rahman Q. The neurodevelopment of human sexual orientation. Neurosci Biobehav Rev. 2005;29(7):1057-66. Epub 2005 Apr 25. Review. PubMedPMID: 16143171.

Ramirez JM, Tryba AK, Peña F. Pacemaker neurons and neuronal networks: an integrative view. Curr Opin Neurobiol. 2004 Dec;14(6):665-74. Review. PubMed PMID: 15582367.

Ramirez JM, Pearson KG. Octopamine induces bursting and plateau potentials in insect neurones. Brain Res. 1991 May 24;549(2):332-7. PubMed PMID: 1884227.

Rand N, Torok M. [On the way to the secret of Freudian psychoanalysis. From Emmy von N. to "Totem and taboo"]. Psyche (Stuttg). 1993 Sep;47(9):866-81. German. PubMed PMID: 8210450.

Rapoport SI. How did the human brain evolve? A proposal based on new evidence from in vivo brain imaging during attention and ideation. Brain Res Bull. 1999 Oct;50(3):149-65. Review. PubMed PMID: 10566976.

Rapoport SI. Integrated phylogeny of the primate brain, with special reference to humans and their diseases. Brain Res Brain Res Rev. 1990 Sep-Dec;15(3):267-94. Review. PubMed PMID:2289087.

Rapoport SI. Hypothesis: Alzheimer's disease is a phylogenetic disease. Med Hypotheses. 1989 Jul;29(3):147-50. PubMed PMID:2528670.

Rapoport SI. Brain evolution and Alzheimer's disease. Rev Neurol (Paris). 1988;144(2):79-90. Review. PubMed PMID:2898165.

Reid VM, Hoehl S, Striano T. The perception of biological motion by infants: an event-related potential study. Neurosci Lett. 2006 Mar 13;395(3):211-4. Epub 2005 Nov 18. PubMed PMID: 16298485.

Reilly KT, Sirigu A. The motor cortex and its role in phantom limb phenomena. Neuroscientist. 2008 Apr;14(2):195-202. Epub 2007 Nov 7. Review. PubMed PMID: 17989169.

Reilly KT, Mercier C, Schieber MH, Sirigu A. Persistent hand motor commands in the amputees' brain. Brain. 2006 Aug;129(Pt 8):2211-23. Epub 2006 Jun 24. PubMed PMID: 16799174.

Reinke KR. Leonardo Da Vinci's right-to-left "mirrored" writing revisited. Ann Plast Surg. 1993 Jan;30(1):89-92. PubMed PMID:8333692.

Richmond BG, Strait DS. Evidence that humans evolved from a knuckle-walking ancestor. Nature. 2000 Mar 23;404(6776):382-5. PubMed PMID: 10746723.

Ridley RM. The psychology of perserverative and stereotyped behaviour. Prog Neurobiol. 1994 Oct;44(2):221-31. Review. PubMed PMID:7831478.

Rilling JK, Insel TR. The primate neocortex in comparative perspective using magnetic resonance imaging. J Hum Evol. 1999 Aug;37(2):191-223. PubMed PMID: 10444351.

Rilling JK, Insel TR. Differential expansion of neural projection systems in primate brain evolution. Neuroreport. 1999 May 14;10(7):1453-9. PubMed PMID: 10380962.

Rilling JK, Insel TR. Evolution of the cerebellum in primates: differences in relative volume among monkeys, apes and humans. Brain Behav Evol. 1998;52(6):308-14. PubMed PMID:9807015.

Ritchie JB, Carlson T. Mirror, mirror, on the wall, is that even my hand at all? Changes in the afterimage of one's reflection in a mirror in response to bodily movement. Neuropsychologia. 2010 Apr;48(5):1495-500. Epub 2010 Feb 1. PubMed PMID: 20117118.

Roberts M. Gilles Deleuze: psychiatry, subjectivity, and the passive synthesis of time. Nurs Philos. 2006 Oct;7(4):191-204. PubMed PMID: 16965301.

Robertson RM, Pearson KG. Neural circuits in the flight system of the locust. J Neurophysiol. 1985 Jan;53(1):110-28. PubMed PMID:2983035.

Robertson RM, Pearson KG. Interneurons in the flight system of thelocust: distribution, connections, and resetting properties. J Comp Neurol. 1983 Mar 20;215(1):33-50. PubMed PMID: 6853764.

Robinson DL, McClurkin JW. The visual superior colliculus and pulvinar.Rev Oculomot Res. 1989;3:337-60. Review. PubMed PMID:2486329.

Robinson R. "New Functional Imaging Study of PVS Sheds LIght on Nature of Consciousness" in Neurology Today 2010 Feb: 10(3):12-13

Rodier PM, Ingram JL, Tisdale B, Croog VJ. Linking etiologies in humans and animal models: studies of autism. Reprod Toxicol. 1997 Mar-Jun;11(2-3):417-22. Review. PubMed PMID:9100317.

Rodier PM, Ingram JL, Tisdale B, Nelson S, Romano J. Embryological origin for autism: developmental anomalies of the cranial nerve motor nuclei. J Comp Neurol. 1996 Jun 24;370(2):247-61. PubMed PMID:8808733.

Roesch TA. Why we really do need Ritalin. Pediatrics. 1998 Jan;101(1Pt 1):161. PubMed PMID: 11345985.

Rojahn J, Matson JL, Lott D, Esbensen AJ, Smalls Y. The Behavior Problems Inventory: an instrument for the assessment of self-injury, stereotyped behavior, and aggression/destruction in individuals with developmental disabilities. J Autism Dev Disord. 2001 Dec;31(6):577-88. PubMed PMID:11814269.

Romano M. A model of speech-locomotory merger and its implications for the protohuman evolutionary ecology. Ann Ig. 1992 Jan-Feb;4(1):51-64. PubMed PMID: 1283072.

Rosen HJ, Cummings J. A real reason for patients with pseudobulbar affectto smile. Ann Neurol. 2007 Feb;61(2):92-6. Review. PubMed PMID:17212357.

Rosenberg PB, Rosse R. Impulsive suicide attempts by a patient with alcoholic dementia. Psychosomatics. 2003 Sep-Oct;44(5):415-6. PubMed PMID: 12954917.

Rosse R, Deutsch S, Chilton M. Cocaine addicts prone to cocaine-induced psychosis have lower body mass index than cocaine addicts resistant to cocaine-induced psychosis--Implications for the cocaine model of psychosis proneness. Isr J Psychiatry Relat Sci. 2005;42(1):45-50. PubMed PMID: 16134406.

Rosse R, Ciolino C. Dopamine agonists and neuroleptic malignant syndrome. AmJ Psychiatry. 1985 Feb;142(2):270-1. PubMed PMID:3970258.

Rosse RB, Deutsch SI. The "Yoking" of glutamatergic brain mechanisms involved in controlling brain neuronal excitability and psychosis to brain mechanisms involved in appetite regulation: a new hypothesis on the origin of psychosis. Med Hypotheses. 2004;62(3):406-12. PubMed PMID: 14975512.

Rudan V, Tripković M, Vidas M. The application of psychoanalytic principles to the study of "magic". Coll Antropol. 2003 Jun;27(1):403-11. PubMed PMID: 12974171.

Ruiz RE, Hall BL, Doyle C, Ward FE. Baboon and cotton-top tamarin B2m cDNA sequences and the evolution of primate beta 2-microglobulin. Hum Immunol. 1994 Mar;39(3):188-94. PubMed PMID: 8026986.

Sabbagh MA. Understanding orbitofrontal contributions to theory-of-mind reasoning: implications for autism. Brain Cogn. 2004 Jun;55(1):209-19. Review. PubMed PMID: 15134854.

Sachdev PS, Malhi GS. Obsessive-compulsive behaviour: a disorder of decision-making. Aust N Z J Psychiatry. 2005 Sep;39(9):757-63. Review. PubMed PMID: 16168033.

Sainburg RL. Evidence for a dynamic-dominance hypothesis of handedness. Exp Brain Res. 2002 Jan;142(2):241-58. Epub 2001 Nov 22. PubMed PMID: 11807578.

Saint-Cyr JA, Taylor AE, Nicholson K. Behavior and the basal ganglia. Adv Neurol. 1995;65:1-28. Review. PubMed PMID: 7872134.

Salter JE, Roy EA, Black SE, Joshi A, Almeida Q. Gestural imitation and limb apraxia in corticobasal degeneration. Brain Cogn. 2004 Jul;55(2):400-2. PubMed PMID: 15177822.

Samsonovich AV, Ascoli GA. The conscious self: ontology, epistemology andthe mirror quest. Cortex. 2005 Oct;41(5):621-36; discussion 731-4. Review. PubMed PMID: 16209326.

Sarnat HB, Netsky MG. When does a ganglion become a brain? Evolutionary origin of the central nervous system. Semin Pediatr Neurol. 2002 Dec;9(4):240-53. Review. PubMed PMID: 12523550.

Sarnat HB, Netsky MG. Hypothesis: Phylogenetic diseases of the nervous system. Can J Neurol Sci. 1984 Feb;11(1):29-33. PubMed PMID: 6704791.

Saugstad LF. From superior adaptation and function to brain dysfunction--the neglect of epigenetic factors. Nutr Health. 2004;18(1):3-27. Review. PubMedPMID: 15615323.

Saugstad LF. A lack of cerebral lateralization in schizophrenia is within the normal variation in brain maturation but indicates late, slow maturation. Schizophr Res. 1999 Oct 19;39(3):183-96. Review. PubMed PMID: 10507511.

Sax L. What was the cause of Nietzsche's dementia? J Med Biogr. 2003 Feb;11(1):47-54. PubMed PMID: 12522502.

Scarmeas N, Brandt J, Albert M, Hadjigeorgiou G, Papadimitriou A, Dubois B, Sarazin M, Devanand D, Honig L, Marder K, Bell K, Wegesin D, Blacker D, Stern Y. Delusions and hallucinations are associated with worse outcome in Alzheimer disease. Arch Neurol. 2005 Oct;62(10):1601-8. PubMed PMID: 16216946.

Schneider SP, Fyffe RE. Involvement of GABA and glycine in recurrent inhibition of spinal motoneurons. J Neurophysiol. 1992 Aug;68(2):397-406. PubMed PMID: 1326603.

Schott GD. Some neurological observations on Leonardo da Vinci's handwriting. J Neurol Sci. 1979 Aug;42(3):321-9. PubMed PMID: 390099.

Schredl M. Continuity between waking life and dreaming: are all waking activities reflected equally often in dreams? Percept Mot Skills. 2000 Jun;90(3 Pt 1):844-6. PubMed PMID: 10883763.

Schwartz BL, Mastropaolo J, Rosse RB, Mathis G, Deutsch SI. Imitation of facial expressions in schizophrenia. Psychiatry Res. 2006 Dec 7;145(2-3):87-94. Epub 2006 Oct 30. PubMed PMID: 17074400.

Schürmann M, Hesse MD, Stephan KE, Saarela M, Zilles K, Hari R, Fink GR. Yearning to yawn: the neural basis of contagious yawning. Neuroimage. 2005 Feb 15;24(4):1260-4. PubMed PMID: 15670705.

Schütz-Bosbach S, Mancini B, Aglioti SM, Haggard P. Self and other in the human motor system. Curr Biol. 2006 Sep 19;16(18):1830-4. PubMed PMID: 16979561.

Seeley WW, Crawford RK, Zhou J, Miller BL, Greicius MD. Neurodegenerative diseases target large-scale human brain networks. Neuron. 2009 Apr 16;62(1):42-52. PubMed PMID: 19376066; PubMed Central PMCID:PMC2691647.

Seeley WW. Selective functional, regional, and neuronal vulnerability in frontotemporal dementia. Curr Opin Neurol. 2008 Dec;21(6):701-7. Review.PubMed PMID: 18989116.

Seeley WW, Carlin DA, Allman JM, Macedo MN, Bush C, Miller BL, Dearmond SJ. Early frontotemporal dementia targets neurons unique to apes and humans. Ann Neurol. 2006 Dec;60(6):660-7. PubMed PMID: 17187353.

Sehgal A. Molecular genetic analysis of circadian rhythms in vertebrates and invertebrates. Curr Opin Neurobiol. 1995 Dec;5(6):824-31. Review. PubMedPMID: 8805416.

Seidman LJ, Valera EM, Makris N. Structural brain imaging of attention-deficit/hyperactivity disorder. Biol Psychiatry. 2005 Jun 1;57(11):1263-72. Epub 2005 Jan 22. Review. PubMed PMID: 15949998.

Semendeferi K, Armstrong E, Schleicher A, Zilles K, Van Hoesen GW. Prefrontal cortex in humans and apes: a comparative study of area 10. Am J Phys Anthropol. 2001 Mar;114(3):224-41. PubMed PMID: 11241188.

Sergent C, Dehaene S. Neural processes underlying conscious perception: experimental findings and a global neuronal workspace framework. J Physiol Paris. 2004 Jul-Nov;98(4-6):374-84. Epub 2005 Nov 15. Review. PubMed PMID: 16293402.

Serra-Pinheiro MA, Schmitz M, Mattos P, Souza I. [Oppositional defiant disorder: a review of neurobiological and environmental correlates, comorbidities, treatment and prognosis]. Rev Bras Psiquiatr. 2004 Dec;26(4):273-6. Epub 2005 Feb 23. Review. Portuguese. Erratum in: Rev Bras Psiquiatr. 2005 Mar;27(1):iii-iv. PubMed PMID: 15729463.

Sevush S. Single-neuron theory of consciousness. J Theor Biol. 2006 Feb 7;238(3):704-25. Epub 2005 Aug 3. PubMed PMID: 16083912.

Shalev RS, Manor O, Kerem B, Ayali M, Badichi N, Friedlander Y, Gross-TsurV. Developmental dyscalculia is a familial learning disability. J Learn Disabil.2001 Jan-Feb;34(1):59-65. PubMed PMID: 15497272.

Shavitt RG, Hounie AG, Rosário Campos MC, Miguel EC. Tourette's Syndrome. Psychiatr Clin North Am. 2006 Jun;29(2):471-86. Review. PubMed PMID:16650718.

Shelley-Tremblay JF, Rosén LA. Attention deficit hyperactivity disorder: an evolutionary perspective. J Genet Psychol. 1996 Dec;157(4):443-53.Review. PubMed PMID: 8955426.

Sheridan PL, Solomont J, Kowall N, Hausdorff JM. Influence of executive function on locomotor function: divided attention increases gait variability in Alzheimer's disease. J Am Geriatr Soc. 2003 Nov;51(11):1633-7. PubMed PMID: 14687395.

Shoshani J, Groves CP, Simons EL, Gunnell GF. Primate phylogeny: morphological vs. molecular results. Mol Phylogenet Evol. 1996 Feb;5(1):102-54. Review. PubMed PMID: 8673281.

Sian J, Dexter DT, Lees AJ, Daniel S, Jenner P, Marsden CD.Glutathione-related enzymes in brain in Parkinson's disease. Ann Neurol.1994 Sep;36(3):356-61. PubMed PMID: 8080243.

Silva RR, Muñoz DM, Daniel W, Barickman J, Friedhoff AJ. Causes of haloperidol discontinuation in patients with Tourette's disorder: management and alternatives. J Clin Psychiatry. 1996 Mar;57(3):129-35. PubMed PMID:8617698.

Skinner FK, Mulloney B. Intersegmental coordination in invertebrates and vertebrates. Curr Opin Neurobiol. 1998 Dec;8(6):725-32. Review. PubMedPMID: 9914235.

Skoyles JR. Human balance, the evolution of bipedalism and dysequilibrium syndrome. Med Hypotheses.2006;66(6):1060-8. Epub 2006 Mar 13. PubMedPMID: 16530977.

Slater J, Hunt HT. Postural-vestibular integration and forms of dreaming: a preliminary report on the effects of brief T'ai Chi Chuan training. Percept Mot Skills. 1997 Aug;85(1):97-8. PubMed PMID: 9293563.

Slocombe KE, Zuberbühler K. Functionally referential communication in a chimpanzee. Curr Biol. 2005 Oct 11;15(19):1779-84. PubMed PMID:16213827.

Slocombe KE, Newton-Fisher NE. Fruit sharing between wild adult chimpanzees (Pan troglodytes schweinfurthii): a socially significant event? Am J Primatol. 2005 Apr;65(4):385-91. PubMed PMID:15834886.

Slocombe KE, Zuberbühler K. Agonistic screams in wild chimpanzees (Pan troglodytes schweinfurthii) vary as a function of social role. J Comp Psychol. 2005 Feb;119(1):67-77. PubMed PMID:15740431.

Smith JC. Angelman syndrome: evolution of the phenotype in adolescents and adults. Dev Med Child Neurol. 2001 Jul;43(7):476-80. PubMed PMID:11463179.

Smith MC, Smith MK, Ellgring H. Spontaneous and posed facial expression in Parkinson's disease. J Int Neuropsychol Soc. 1996 Sep;2(5):383-91. PubMed PMID: 9375163.

Smythies J. The functional neuroanatomy of awareness: with a focus on the role of various anatomical systems in the control of intermodal attention. Conscious Cogn. 1997 Dec;6(4):455-81. Review. PubMed PMID: 9479480.

Solomon J. in Montagu A, *Touching* Harper and Row Third Edition New York 1986

Soltis J. The signal functions of early infant crying. Behav Brain Sci. 2004 Aug;27(4):443-58; discussion 459-90. PubMed PMID: 15773426.

Son EJ, Bang JH, Kang JG. Anterior inferior cerebellar artery infarction presenting with sudden hearing loss and vertigo. Laryngoscope. 2007 Mar;117(3):556-8. PubMed PMID: 17334322.

South ST, Swensen JJ, Maxwell T, Rope A, Brothman AR, Chen Z. A new genomic mechanism leading to cri-du-chat syndrome. Am J Med Genet A. 2006 Dec 15;140(24):2714-20. PubMed PMID: 17103439.

Spengler A. Manifest sadomasochism of males: results of an empirical study. Arch Sex Behav. 1977 Nov;6(6):441-56. PubMed PMID: 931623.

Squire LR, Zola SM. Amnesia, memory and brain systems. Philos Trans R Soc Lond B Biol Sci. 1997 Nov 29;352(1362):1663-73. Review. PubMed PMID: 9415918; PubMed Central PMCID: PMC1692096.

Squire LR, Zola SM. Structure and function of declarative and nondeclarative memory systems. Proc Natl Acad Sci U S A. 1996 Nov 26;93(24):13515-22. Review. PubMed PMID: 8942965; PubMed Central PMCID: PMC33639.

Stanford CB. Arboreal bipedalism in wild chimpanzees: implications for the evolution of hominid posture and locomotion. Am J Phys Anthropol. 2006 Feb;129(2):225-31. PubMed PMID: 16288480.

Stein R. Why perversion?: 'False love' and the perverse pact. Int J Psychoanal. 2005 Jun;86(Pt 3):776-99. PubMed PMID: 16096075.

Steudel-Numbers KL. Energetics in Homo erectus and other early hominins: the consequences of increased lower-limb length. J Hum Evol. 2006 Nov;51(5):445-53. Epub 2006 May 7. PubMed PMID: 16780923.

Stevens CF. An evolutionary scaling law for the primate visual system and its basis in cortical function. Nature. 2001 May 10;411(6834):193-5. PubMed PMID: 11346795.

Stone VE, Baron-Cohen S, Knight RT. Frontal lobe contributions to theory of mind. J Cogn Neurosci. 1998 Sep;10(5):640-56. PubMed PMID: 9802997.

Streit J, Tscherter A, Heuschkel MO, Renaud P. The generation of rhythmic activity in dissociated cultures of rat spinal cord. Eur J Neurosci. 2001 Jul;14(2):191-202. PubMed PMID: 11553272.

Sturm VE, Ascher EA, Miller BL, Levenson RW. Diminished self-conscious emotional responding in frontotemporal lobar degeneration patients. Emotion. 2008 Dec;8(6):861-9. PubMed PMID: 19102597; PubMed Central PMCID: PMC2733345.

Sugar M. Commonalities between the Isaac and Oedipus myths: a speculation. J Am Acad Psychoanal. 2002 Winter;30(4):691-706. PubMed PMID: 12597111.

Sunderland A. Impaired imitation of meaningless gestures in ideomotor apraxia: a conceptual problem not a disorder of action control? A single case investigation. Neuropsychologia. 2007 Apr 9;45(8):1621-31. Epub 2007 Jan 20. PubMed PMID: 17306847.

Suzuki K. Civilization, culture and neurotic depression: in view of the Freudian theory. Psychiatry Clin Neurosci. 1995 Dec;49(5-6):255-8. PubMed PMID: 8726109.

Symons FJ, Tapp J, Wulfsberg A, Sutton KA, Heeth WL, Bodfish JW. Sequential analysis of the effects of naltrexone on the environmental mediation of self-injurious behavior. Exp Clin Psychopharmacol. 2001 Aug;9(3):269-76. PubMed PMID: 11534537.

Synofzik M, Vosgerau G, Newen A. I move, therefore I am: a new theoretical framework to investigate agency and ownership. Conscious Cogn. 2008 Jun;17(2):411-24. Epub 2008 Apr 14. PubMed PMID: 18411059.

Tan U. Evidence for "Uner Tan Syndrome" as a human model for reverse evolution. Int J Neurosci. 2006 Dec;116(12):1539-47. PubMed PMID: 17145687.

Tan U. Evidence for "Unertan Syndrome" and the evolution of the human mind. Int J Neurosci. 2006 Jul;116(7):763-74. PubMed PMID: 16861146.

Tassinari CA, Rubboli G, Gardella E, Cantalupo G, Calandra-Buonaura G, Vedovello M, Alessandria M, Gandini G, Cinotti S, Zamponi N, Meletti S. Central pattern generators for a common semiology in fronto-limbic seizures and in parasomnias. A neuroethologic approach. Neurol Sci. 2005 Dec;26 Suppl 3:s225-32. Review. PubMed PMID: 16331401.

Teitelbaum O, Benton T, Shah PK, Prince A, Kelly JL, Teitelbaum P. Eshkol-Wachman movement notation in diagnosis: the early detection of Asperger's syndrome. Proc Natl Acad Sci U S A. 2004 Aug 10;101(32):11909-14. Epub 2004 Jul 28. PubMed PMID: 15282371; PubMed Central PMCID: PMC511073.

Teitelbaum P. A proposed primate animal model of autism. Eur Child Adolesc Psychiatry. 2003 Jan;12(1):48-9. PubMed PMID: 12601565.

Teitelbaum P, Teitelbaum O, Nye J, Fryman J, Maurer RG. Movement analysis in infancy may be useful for early diagnosis of autism. Proc Natl Acad Sci U S A. 1998 Nov 10;95(23):13982-7. PubMed PMID: 9811912; PubMed Central PMCID:

Thompson T, Hackenberg T, Cerutti D, Baker D, Axtell S. Opioid antagonist effects on self-injury in adults with mental retardation: response form and location as determinants of medication effects. Am J Ment Retard. 1994 Jul;99(1):85-102. PubMed PMID: 7946257.

Timmann D, Watts S, Hore J. Causes of left-right ball inaccuracy in overarm throws made by cerebellar patients. Exp Brain Res. 2000 Feb;130(4):441-52. PubMedPMID: 10717787.

Tofaris GK, Revesz T, Jacques TS, Papacostas S, Chataway J. Adult-onset neurodegeneration with brain iron accumulation and cortical alpha-synuclein and tau pathology: a distinct clinicopathological entity. Arch Neurol. 2007 Feb;64(2):280-2. PubMed PMID: 17296847.

Treffert DA. The savant syndrome: an extraordinary condition. A synopsis: past, present, future. Philos Trans R Soc Lond B Biol Sci. 2009 May 27;364(1522):1351-7. Review. PubMed PMID: 19528017; PubMed Central PMCID: PMC2677584.

Treffert DA, Christensen DD. Inside the mind of a savant. Sci Am. 2005 Dec;293(6):108-13. PubMed PMID: 16323698.

Treffert DA, Wallace GL. Islands of genius. Artistic brilliance and a dazzling memory can sometimes accompany autism and other developmental disorders. Sci Am. 2002 Jun;286(6):76-85. PubMed PMID: 12030094.454.

Treffert DA. The savant syndrome and autistic disorder. CNS Spectr. 1999 Dec;4(12):57-60. PubMed PMID: 18311109.

Trémeau F, Malaspina D, Duval F, Corrêa H, Hager-Budny M, Coin-Bariou L, Macher JP, Gorman JM. Facial expressiveness in patients with schizophrenia compared to depressed patients and nonpatient comparison subjects. Am J Psychiatry. 2005 Jan;162(1):92-101. PubMed PMID: 15625206.

Tsakiris M, Schütz-Bosbach S, Gallagher S. On agency and body-ownership: phenomenological and neurocognitive reflections. Conscious Cogn. 2007 Sep;16(3):645-60. Epub 2007 Jul 9. Review. PubMed PMID: 17616469.

Tutté JC. The concept of psychical trauma: a bridge in interdisciplinary space. Int J Psychoanal. 2004 Aug;85(Pt 4):897-921. Review. PubMed PMID: 15310427.

Vallortigara G, Rogers LJ. Survival with an asymmetrical brain: advantages and disadvantages of cerebral lateralization. Behav Brain Sci. 2005 Aug;28(4):575-89; discussion 589-633. Review. PubMed PMID: 16209828.

Vallortigara G, Rogers LJ, Bisazza A. Possible evolutionary origins of cognitive brain lateralization. Brain Res Brain Res Rev. 1999 Aug;30(2):164-75. Review. PubMed PMID: 10525173.

van den Heuvel OA, Veltman DJ, Groenewegen HJ, Cath DC, van Balkom AJ, van Hartskamp J, Barkhof F, van Dyck R. Frontal-striatal dysfunction during planning in obsessive-compulsive disorder. Arch Gen Psychiatry. 2005 Mar;62(3):301-9.

van der Kolk BA, Spinazzola J, Blaustein ME, Hopper JW, Hopper EK, Korn DL, Simpson WB. A randomized clinical trial of eye movement desensitization and reprocessing (EMDR), fluoxetine, and pill placebo in the treatment of posttraumatic stress disorder: treatment effects and long-term maintenance. J Clin Psychiatry. 2007 Jan;68(1):37-46. PubMed PMID: 17284128.

Vetrugno R, Liguori R, Cortelli P, Plazzi G, Vicini C, Campanini A, D'Angelo R, Provini F, Montagna P. Sleep-related stridor due to dystonic vocal cord motion and neurogenic tachypnea/tachycardia in multiple system atrophy. Mov Disord.2007 Apr 15;22(5):673-8. PubMed PMID: 17266093.

Videan EN, McGrew WC. Bipedality in chimpanzee (Pan troglodytes) and bonobo (Pan paniscus): testing hypotheses on the evolution of bipedalism. Am J Phys Anthropol. 2002 Jun;118(2):184-90. PubMed PMID: 12012370.

Vincent A, Baruch P, Pourcher E, Vincent EP. [Involvement of the basal ganglia in obsessive compulsive disorder: a review]. Can J Psychiatry. 1994 Nov;39(9):545-50. Review. French. PubMed PMID: 7874656.

Voderholzer U, Riemann D, Huwig-Poppe C, Kuelz AK, Kordon A, Bruestle K, Berger M, Hohagen F. Sleep in obsessive compulsive disorder: polysomnographic studies under baseline conditions and after experimentally induced serotonin deficiency. Eur Arch Psychiatry Clin Neurosci. 2007 Apr;257(3):173-82. Epub 2006 Dec 5. PubMed PMID: 17149537.

Vogeley K, Bussfeld P, Newen A, Herrmann S, Happé F, Falkai P, Maier W, Shah NJ, Fink GR, Zilles K. Mind reading: neural mechanisms of theory of mind and self-perspective. Neuroimage. 2001 Jul;14(1 Pt 1):170-81. PubMed PMID: 11525326.

Völlm BA, Taylor AN, Richardson P, Corcoran R, Stirling J, McKie S, Deakin JF, Elliott R. Neuronal correlates of theory of mind and empathy: a functional magnetic resonance imaging study in a nonverbal task. Neuroimage. 2006 Jan 1;29(1):90-8. Epub 2005 Aug 24. PubMed PMID: 16122944.

Walusinski O. Yawning: unsuspected avenue for a better understanding of arousal and interoception. Med Hypotheses. 2006;67(1):6-14. Epub 2006 Mar 7. PubMed PMID: 16520004.

Watanabe H, Fujiyama A, Hattori M, Taylor TD, Toyoda A, Kuroki Y, Noguchi H, BenKahla A, Lehrach H, Sudbrak R, Kube M, Taenzer S, Galgoczy P, Platzer M, Scharfe M, Nordsiek G, Blöcker H, Hellmann I, Khaitovich P, Pääbo S, Reinhardt R, Zheng HJ, Zhang XL, Zhu GF, Wang BF, Fu G, Ren SX, Zhao GP, Chen Z, Lee YS, Cheong JE, Choi SH, Wu KM, Liu TT, Hsiao KJ, Tsai SF, Sakaki Y. DNA sequence an comparative analysis of chimpanzee chromosome 22. Nature. 2004 May 27;429(6990):382-8. PubMed PMID: 15164055.

Watson NV, Kimura D. Right-hand superiority for throwing but not for intercepting. Neuropsychologia. 1989;27(11-12):1399-414. PubMed PMID: 2615939.

Weeks RA, Ceballos-Baumann A, Piccini P, Boecker H, Harding AE, BrooksDJ. Cortical control of movement in Huntington's disease. A PET activation study. Brain. 1997 Sep;120 (Pt 9):1569-78. PubMed PMID: 9313640.

Weiden P, Bruun R. Worsening of Tourette's disorder due toneuroleptic-induced akathisia. Am J Psychiatry. 1987 Apr;144(4):504-5.PubMed PMID: 2882696.

Weiss B, Landrigan PJ. The developing brain and the environment: an introduction. Environ Health Perspect. 2000 Jun;108 Suppl 3:373-4. PubMed PMID: 10852830; PubMed Central PMCID: PMC1637828.

Wenderoth N, Debaere F, Sunaert S, Swinnen SP. The role of anterior cingulate cortex and precuneus in the coordination of motor behaviour. Eur J Neurosci. 2005 Jul;22(1):235-46. PubMed PMID: 16029213.

Whiting BA, Barton RA. The evolution of the cortico-cerebellar complex in primates: anatomical connections predict patterns of correlated evolution. J Hum Evol. 2003 Jan;44(1):3-10. PubMed PMID: 12604300.

Wilhelm S, Keuthen NJ, Deckersbach T, Engelhard IM, Forker AE, Baer L,O'Sullivan RL, Jenike MA. Self-injurious skin picking: clinical characteristicsand comorbidity. J Clin Psychiatry. 1999 Jul;60(7):454-9. PubMed PMID: 10453800.

Wise SP, Murray EA, Gerfen CR. The frontal cortex-basal ganglia system in primates. Crit Rev Neurobiol. 1996;10(3-4):317-56. Review. PubMed PMID: 8978985.

Wolfe SW, Crisco JJ, Orr CM, Marzke MW. The dart-throwing motion of the wrist: is it unique to humans? J Hand Surg Am. 2006 Nov;31(9):1429-37. PubMed PMID: 17095370.

Wright CV. Mechanisms of left-right asymmetry: what's right and what'sleft? Dev Cell. 2001 Aug;1(2):179-86. PubMed PMID: 11702778.

Wyss D, Laue B. [Oedipus - anthropology of enlightenment and interpretation]. Z Klin Psychol Psychother. 1977;25(1):43-51. German.PubMed PMID: 906616.

Xitco MJ Jr, Gory JD, Kuczaj SA 2nd. Dolphin pointing is linked to the attentional behavior of a receiver. Anim Cogn. 2004 Oct;7(4):231-8. Epub 2004Apr 14. PubMed PMID: 15088149.

Yeo RA, Gangestad SW, Edgar C, Thoma R. The evolutionary genetic underpinnings of schizophrenia: the developmental instability model.Schizophr Res. 1999 Oct 19;39(3):197-206. Review. PubMed PMID: 10507512.

Young C, Brook A. Schopenhauer and Freud. Int J Psychoanal. 1994 Feb;75 (Pt 1):101-18. PubMed PMID: 8005756.

Young RW. Evolution of the human hand: the role of throwing and clubbing. J Anat. 2003 Jan;202(1):165-74. PubMed PMID: 12587931; PubMed Central PMCID: PMC1571064.

Yu H, Sternad D, Corcos DM, Vaillancourt DE. Role of hyperactive cerebellum and motor cortex in Parkinson's disease. Neuroimage. 2007 Mar;35(1):222-33. Epub 2007 Jan 12. PubMed PMID: 17223579; PubMed Central PMCID: PMC1853309.

Zarranz JJ, Gómez-Esteban JC, Atarés B, Lezcano E, Forcadas M.Tau-predominant-associated pathology in a sporadic late-onset Hallervorden-Spatz syndrome. Mov Disord. 2006 Jan;21(1):107-11. PubMed PMID: 16114023.

Zeifman DM. An ethological analysis of human infant crying: answering Tinbergen's four questions. Dev Psychobiol. 2001 Dec;39(4):265-85. PubMedPMID: 11745323.

Photo Credits

Listed in order of appearance as shown in "Illustrations".

ID 145295058 © Volodymyr Melnyk | Dreamstime.com

Man with arms raised ID 32937764 © Aleksminyaylo1 | Dreamstime.com

ID 110374600 © Alina ShpakDreamstime.com

Primitive man and facial expression ID 32560235 © Marcovarro | Dreamstime.com

Bow and arrow and deer ID 109863350 © Aleksandr Gerasimov | Dreamstime.com

Warrior with weapon in each hand ID 24294316 © Romangorielov | Dreamstime.com

Woman with club ID 76282946 © Marcogarrincha | Dreamstime.com

Baby sucking toe ID 138955643 © Matrixximages | Dreamstime.com

Newborn with grasp reflex ID 122396192 © Godsandkings | Dreamstime.com

License info here: https://commons.wikimedia.org/wiki/File:Asymmetrical_tonic_neck_reflex_(ATNR)_in_a_two-week-old_female.jpg#mw-jump-to-license

Fencing ID 59799550 © Everett Collection Inc. | Dreamstime.com

Apes huddling ID 17858929 © Wilfred Stanley Sussenbach | Dreamstime.com

Dog with tennis ball ID 75002872 © Dreamstime Agency | Dreamstime.com

Dog with tongue out and ball ID 75970858 © Ell Langford | Dreamstime.com

Baby with tongue out with ball ID 47644721 © Steven Day | Dreamstime.com

Scared monkey with tongue out ID 15219941 © Steffen Foerster | Dreamstime.com

Tennis swing ID 80268347 © Oleksandr Boiko | Dreamstime.com

Man with Machete ID 104794126 © Andrii Klemenchenko | Dreamstime.com

Polynesian Dance ID 34967141 © Rafael Ben Ari | Dreamstime.com

Submarine pitching ID 4282364 © Paul Hakimata | Dreamstime.com

Overhead pitching ID 18434300 © Lawrence Weslowski Jr | Dreamstime.com

Crouched Hunter in jungle ID 81020712 © Andrey Gudkov | Dreamstime.com

Parkinson also crouched ID 124953968 © Alexugalek | Dreamstime.com

Chimps crouching ID 10135865 © Ksenyalim | Dreamstime.com

Chimps mirror image modelingID 69792672 © Luke Tracy | Dreamstime.com

Senior with arms raised ID 129490914 © Amazingmikael | Dreamstime.com

Overtime

In 2016, 2017 and 2019, four studies have magnified the intertwining of Sports, Neurology, Anthropology and Physical Exercise.

- It has been proposed that physical activity can decrease the risk for getting Parkinson's disease.

  LaHue SC[1], Comella CL[2], Tanner CM[3].Mov Disord. 2016 Oct;31(10):1444-1454. doi: 10.1002/mds.26728. The best medicine? The influence of physical activity and inactivity on Parkinson's disease

- It has been shown that exercise improves the motor and some of the cognitive decline in Parkinson's disease.

  Stuckenschneider T[1,2,] Askew CD[2], Menêses AL[2], Baake R[3], Weber J[1], Schneider S[1,2].J Parkinsons Dis. 2019;9(1):73-95. doi:10.3233/JPD181484. The Effect of Different Exercise Modes on DomainSpecific Cognitive Function in Patients Suffering from Parkinson's Disease:A Systematic Review of Randomized Controlled Trials.

- It has been shown that exercise decreases the risk of dementia.

  Guure CB[1], Ibrahim NA[2], Adam MB[3], Said SM[4].Biomed Res Int. 2017;2017:9016924. doi: 10.1155/2017/9016924. Epub 2017 Feb 7.Impact of Physical Activity on Cognitive Decline, Dementia, and Its Subtypes: Meta-Analysis of Prospective Studies.

- It has also been revealed that physical exercise delays cognitive decline in individuals who have biomarkers for Alzheimer's disease severity (beta amyloid) on brain scans.

  Rabin JS[1,2], Klein H[3], Kirn DR[3,4], Schultz AP[3,5], Yang HS[3,4], Hampton O[3], Jiang S[3], Buckley RF[3,4,6,7], Viswanathan A[8], Hedden T[9], Pruzin J[3], Yau WW[3], Guzmán-Vélez E[1], Quiroz YT[1,3], Properzi M[3], Marshall GA[3,4], Rentz DM[3,4], Johnson KA[3,4,5,10], Sperling RA[3,4,5], Chhatwal JP[3,4].JAMA Neurol. 2019 Jul 16. doi: 10.1001/jamaneurol.2019.1879. [Epub ahead of print] Associations of Physical Activity and β-Amyloid With Longitudinal Cognition and Neurodegeneration in Clinically Normal Older Adults.

It has been shown that exercise improves the motor and some of the cognitive decline in Parkinson's disease

If in fact we can recapture a healthier state of brain-mind (via improved grey and white matter integrity) through sports with survival our ultimate goal, then the backbone of sports, physical exercise, would link this life maintenance mission to a mitigation of some brain degeneration features.

In a certain sense, Parkinson's and Alzheimer's represent a consequence of brain decay which can to a certain degree be improved upon through aerobic and non-aerobic exercise.

Exercise does not equal sports. Indeed, exercise described in these studies is not linked to individual or group games or overarching team institutions. However, it is the physical exertion that is the ultimate retrogressive activity in the wild particularly during the hunt that we draw upon at the gyms. Mollifying age related declines in thinking and motoric function (AD and PD phenomena) speaks to some regenerative capacity inherent in exercise (possibly mimicked via stem cell activation-related to future stem cell Rx).

Through exercise, our descent into freezing of thought and motion is improved upon. Thus, exercise can free us to engage in the liberating rush (in part due to an endorphin surge) of sports participation itself.

As noted earlier, our brain evolution predisposed us to Parkinson's and Alzheimer's. A drive to survive via exercise would appear to be fighting this biological destiny. Now it should be noted that the mechanism for improvement in PD and AD through exercise is not clear. Forces are unleashed beyond our current rudimentary understanding of brain tissue findings in these conditions (for example the alpha synuclein and beta amyloid deposition noted in PD and AD respectively). Exactly what is occurring microscopically, chemically and physiologically to delay disease appearance and severity is in the speculative domain. Put another way, poor brain oxygenation or poor cerebral blood flow cannot explain the onset of PD and AD. Thus, augmenting brain oxygen and perfusion through exercise would hardly constitute a comprehensive treatment for disease processes that would appear to be far more complex.

Yet, as previously referenced, body injury and a head trauma related march to death are also aspects of the sports immersion (see the unfortunate head injury suffered by Olympic diver Greg Louganis prior to water immersion **https://www.youtube.com/ watch?v=L5nqeFWufrE** and these recent terrible deaths of high school football players **https://www.msn.com/ en-us/sports/ncaafb/2-high-school-football-players-die-in-separate-on-field-accidents-across-nation/ar-AAHoKin?ocid=chromentp**). Is Freud's death instinct a competing drive to counter survivability enhancement through exercise? This kind of question is tackled in Book II in this series.

It is fair to note that our nightly sleep induction is a kind of simulated demise. Other than being in engaged in the mysterious dreaming, we are largely vacant of thought *a la* an Alzheimer's patient and locked out of movement as is the predominant manifestation of Parkinson's. The football player sprawled on the ground after a vicious tackle is also immobile as is the boxer knocked out in the ring.

The oblivion and apathy of Alzheimer's is not seen however in other degenerative dementias where bizarre behavior and psychotic ideation can dominate (such as Diffuse Lewy Body Disease and the Frontotemporal Dementias). Of course, Parkinson's also features excessive movement by way of a resting tremor. Other types of involuntary extra motion, chorea, is a major aspect of Huntington's disease (HD), another important degenerative disorder with a far stronger genetic explanation than typical Alzheimer's or Parkinson's. Suicidality is also much more common than in AD or PD.

Is HD our death wish "on steroids" as we dance and swerve into the night, perhaps lowering any impact of any co-existing AD or PD by way of excess movement and some sort of reach towards physical exercise via the chorea?

It's all rather complicated and replete with hypotheses.

However, our primal neuroanthropology with an attendant neuro-sports hypothesis remains. We cannot compartmentalize our birth, our life activity script and our physical/mental deterioration from a host of cognitive, behavioral and movement issues that are so much a part of human development, history, neurological conditions and sports. A multitude of such intriguing relationships await further elucidation but the primary goal of this book has been to express the fact that such ties exist and can be prominent.

As a premonitory summary to be expounded upon in Book ll, here is a link to a New York Jet football player participating in a game distraction from his "day job" game distraction called professional football.

Brian Winters shows us the remarkably primal neuroanthropological game of axe throwing.

https://www.newyorkjets.com/video/off-the-clock-axe-throwing-with-brian-winters

Evolutionarily, here are some eagles (not the team out of Philadelphia *per se*) scrapping with what looks like a vulture over a fumbled "loose ball" in the form of a fish.

https://www.msn.com/en-us/video/animals/eagles-arguing-over-fish-caught-on-camera/vi-AAHoGv6?ocid=chromentp

Enjoy these videos!! See you in the upcoming Round 2:

PRIMAL SPORTS II—A PSYCHOANALYTICAL, NEUROSOCIOLOGICAL, NEW GAMES, MYTH AND SATIRE LADEN TREATISE— by *Kenneth Bruce Van Gross, MD*

******

About the Author

KENNETH BRUCE VAN GROSS, MD is a neurologist, medical educator and healthcare commentator who has lectured extensively on the Sports-Neurology interface, the aging brain and various subjects in Medicine and Neurology. In 1995, he founded Fusion Clinical Multimedia, Inc. to launch a medical and general education company dedicated to the precise modality and content embraced within *Primal Neuroanthropology*©—*A NeuroSports Hypothesis*, i.e. cross-specialty analysis and idea synthesis derived from a dual discipline approach. With this tome, Neurology and Anthropology serve as the starting blocks for a fascinating and pioneering view of Sports, exploding that linkage to encompass a multiplicity of related fields.

www.ingramcontent.com/pod-product-compliance
Lightning Source LLC
Chambersburg PA
CBHW071237020426
42333CB00015B/1509